# Christopher Marlowe's
# DOCTOR FAUSTUS

## AND

### THE JEW OF MALTA
### EDWARD THE SECOND
### TAMBURLAINE THE GREAT, PART I AND II

**PETER F. MULLANY**
ASSISTANT PROFESSOR OF ENGLISH
MARQUETTE UNIVERSITY

MONARCH
PRESS

*Published by*
*MONARCH PRESS*
*a Simon & Schuster division of*
*Gulf & Western Corporation*
*Simon & Schuster Building*
*1230 Avenue of the Americas*
*New York, N.Y. 10020*
*MONARCH PRESS and colophon are trademarks of Simon*
*& Schuster, registered in the U.S. Patent and Trademark*
*Office.*

*Standard Book Number: 0-671-00717-3*

*Library of Congress Catalog Card Number: 66-1769*

*Printed in the United States of America*

# CONTENTS

# INTRODUCTION

**CHRISTOPHER MARLOWE'S LIFE:** Christopher Marlowe was born in 1564, the year of Shakespeare's birth, in the city of Canterbury. Records indicate that Marlowe was baptized on the twenty-sixth day of February. Marlowe's family was a prosperous one, and his father was a member of the Shoemaker's Guild. Before he was fifteen years old, Christopher Marlowe entered the King's School, Canterbury on a scholarship, and slightly less than two years later he went to Corpus Christi College, Cambridge. As a recipient of an Archbishop Matthew Parker Scholarship to Cambridge, it was expected that Marlowe would take holy orders and enter the clergy.

Marlowe took his Bachelor of Arts degree in 1584 and by 1587 it was acknowledged that he had earned the Master of Arts degree; however, the university authorities refused to grant the Master's degree. The Queen's Privy Council intervened to deny a report that Marlowe had gone beyond the seas to Rheims, and the Council went on to state "Because it was not her Majesty's pleasure that any one employed as he had been in matters touching the benefit of his Country should be defamed by those that are ignorant in th' affairs he went about." The University withdrew its refusal and granted the degree to Marlowe. The University's initial refusal undoubtedly stemmed from a suspicion that Marlowe had converted to Roman Catholicism, for Rheims was at the time a center for English Catholics and for political disaffection. This suspicion may well have been heightened by Marlowe's refusal to take orders in the Anglican Church. At any rate the interference by the government in Marlowe's behalf in the degree matter and the Privy Council's document clearly indicate that Marlowe was engaged on a mission of some political importance. Though the exact nature of the mission is unknown, Marlowe may at this time have had some connection with the elaborate espionage network that Elizabeth had operating abroad to maintain a close watch on Catholic activities.

**LITERARY CAREER:**    Christopher Marlowe's literary career spans the period 1587-1593, six years in which he was to establish himself as a major poet and dramatist. His first dramatic association seems to have been with the Lord Admiral's Men, a dramatic company, which produced his play *Tamburlaine,* which brought to the English popular stage a superman hero motivated by the "thirst of reign and sweetness of a crown." This play was such a popular success that Marlowe wrote a sequel titled *Tamburlaine, Part II*: both plays were printed together in 1590. Lord Strange's Men produced Marlowe's next two plays, *The Jew of Malta* and *The Massacre at Paris. The Jew of Malta* may be dated between 1589 and 1593. Lord Pembroke's Men produced *Edward II* which was probably written in 1591 or 1592. The same company probably produced *Doctor Faustus* which was written in late 1592 or early in 1593. Marlowe's other works include *Dido Queen of Carthage,* a play based closely on Virgil's *Aeneid. Dido* may have been written during Marlowe's Cambridge days. While a student at Cambridge, Marlowe translated the *Amores* of Ovid and the first book of Lucan's *Pharsalia*. He is also the author of a lengthy narrative poem *Hero and Leander* which was completed by Marlowe's friend and fellow poet-dramatist George Chapman. *Hero and Leander,* together with Shakespeare's *Venus and Adonis* and his *The Rape of Lucrece,* are outstanding examples of a type of erotic poetry which became fashionable in the later years of the Elizabethan period.

**THE BRADLEY AFFAIR:**    In September 1589, Marlowe and a friend named Thomas Watson were involved in a sword-fight in which Watson killed a man named William Bradley, who was the son of an innkeeper. It seems that Bradley had cause to suspect Watson because he had asked the authorities for "sureties" (assurances) of the peace against Watson. The upshot of the affair was that Marlowe and Bradley were acquitted after stays of one week and five months respectively in Newgate Prison. It was the judgment of the authorities that Watson, who fatally stabbed Bradley, had acted in self-defense. The episode is important because it marks the beginning of Marlowe's involvement with legal authorities and opens the dramatic series of events which led to his mysterious murder in a tavern brawl in 1593.

**MARLOWE AND CHARGES OF ATHEISM:** Biographies of Marlowe have often taken an excessively romantic view of his career by emphasizing his "free-thinking spirit." A view of Marlowe as a rebellious Renaissance spirit thrusting against the shackles of accepted belief and authority is largely biographical fiction, the product of biographers with a regard for invention. Much of this view is also caused by a too close identification of Marlowe the man with the dramatic supermen who are his tragic heroes—Faustus and Tamburlaine for example. Atheism in the Renaissance meant an active hostility to God and religion; it identified many types of skeptical or naturalistic thinking. Marlowe was first charged with atheism by Robert Greene in *Perimedes the Blacksmith* (1588), and again in *Groatsworth of Wit* (1592) which was written shortly before Greene's death. Greene, like Marlowe, was an important dramatist of the time and among his works are *Friar Bacon and Friar Bungay; James the Fourth;* and *George a Greene, the Pinner of Wakefield*. The charges of atheism against Marlowe played an important part in the final events of his turbulent life.

**MARLOWE'S DEATH:** On May 12, 1593 Thomas Kyd, dramatist and author of *The Spanish Tragedy* (1590), was arrested and charged with atheism. Kyd was suspected of being involved in political disorder. His quarters were searched and he was put to the torture. Papers of an heretical type were found in Kyd's quarters, and Kyd claimed that the documents belonged to Marlowe, who had shared his quarters in the year 1591. After Marlowe's death in 1593, Kyd wrote two letters to the Lord Keeper, Sir John Puckering, in which he repeated in detail his charges against Marlowe. Kyd said that Marlowe had refused holy orders in the Anglican church and had practiced atheism to such an extent as "to jest at the divine scriptures, gibe at prayers, and strive in argument to frustrate and confute what has been spoken or written by prophets and such holy men." Kyd also connected Marlowe with a "school of atheism" or "school of night," whose members included: Thomas Harriott, a mathematician; George Chapman, the dramatist and poet; Sir Walter Raleigh, an important court figure as well as a leading intellectual of the day; and the poets Matthew Roydon and William Warner.

Thomas Kyd, however, was not the only one to come forward at this time with charges of atheism against Marlowe. A certain Richard Baines, shortly before Marlowe's death, informed the Queen's Privy Council of a lecture that Marlowe had delivered wherein Marlowe uttered such atheistical blasphemies as: "That the first beginning of Religion was only to keep men in awe," and "That Christ was a bastard and his mother dishonest." No matter how unreliable Baines might be, the cumulative weight of the evidence points to the fact that Marlowe had the reputation among his contemporaries of being a religious skeptic and of being unorthodox in his philosophical beliefs.

On May 18, 1593 the Queen's Privy Council issued a warrant for Marlowe's arrest; on May 20, 1593 Marlowe was back in London and was ordered to be in daily attendance upon the Council. Ten days later Marlowe was invited to dinner at Deptford, a short distance from London, at a tavern owned by a widow named Eleanor Bull. Ingram Frizer and Nicholas Skeres, boh swindlers, and Raymond Poley, a double-spy, were present with Marlowe at this dinner. All of these men were connected with an espionage ring run by Walsingham. After a day-long drinking bout, an argument erupted over the reckoning, or bill. When Marlowe attacked Frizer, Frizer retaliated and stabbed Marlowe above the right eye. Marlowe died instantly. This at least was the "official" version, for it seems that Marlowe may well have been lured to a planned assassination. Perhaps something in connection with the espionage activities of Sir Thomas Walsingham may have contributed to Marlowe's death.

**CONTEMPORARY ACCOUNTS OF HIS DEATH:** Contemporary accounts of Marlowe's death viewed it as an example of divine providence punishing a blaspheming atheist. Thomas Beard in his *Theatre of God's Judgements* (1597) charged Marlowe with being an atheist, a poet of scurrility, a blasphemer whose death revealed the justice of God punishing heinous sin. Francis Meres in *Palladis Tamia* (1598) used the Beard account and repeated charges of epicureanism and atheism against Marlowe. Meres added that Marlowe had been killed by a serving-man who was a love-rival. William Vaughn in *Golden*

*Grove* (1600) provided some factual material by mentioning Deptford and a man named Ingram. Yet this account, too, mentioned Marlowe's atheism. One strongly suspects that the inaccuracies of these contemporary accounts could well be attributed to a deliberate plot against Marlowe. Marlowe's murderers were all pardoned, and this further builds the suspicion that Marlowe was the victim of an official government intrigue against his life. But the exact cause of why Marlowe was murdered remains a mystery.

## SUMMARY OF THE IMPORTANT FACTS OF MARLOWE'S LIFE:

1. Christopher Marlowe was born in 1564, the year of William Shakespeare's birth.
2. Marlowe was educated at Cambridge and was involved in difficulties there with the authorities with regard to the granting of his Master of Arts degree in 1587. It seems that Marlowe refused to take holy orders and that he was suspected of "converting" to Roman Catholicism. However, the government authorities intervened in Marlowe's behalf, and the degree was granted. Marlowe, at this time, undoubtedly was active in some form of government service.
3. From 1587 to 1593 Marlowe wrote and produced his plays. He established himself as a major dramatist with *Tamburlaine, Parts I and II, The Jew of Malta, Edward the Second,* and *Doctor Faustus.*
4. Marlowe's death involved considerable intrigue. He was killed on May 30, 1593 in a tavern brawl which may well have been part of a deliberate plot to assassinate Marlowe.
5. Marlowe died at the age of twenty-nine, and it is interesting to note that at this time Shakespeare was just beginning his dramatic career. In many particulars Marlowe gave to the English popular theater the foundation upon which Shakespeare was to build.

# BACKGROUND OF THE PLAY

**1. SOURCES:** Marlowe's *Doctor Faustus* is based on a German prose book titled *Historia von D. Johan Fausten* published in Frankfurt-on-Main in 1587. This work was translated into English within five years as *The Historie of the damnable life, and deserved death of Doctor John Faustus.* The historical Faustus was a strolling scholar who had a reputation for possessing magical powers. He lived during the period 1510-1540, and after his death his fame spread far, and often this fame took a strongly anti-papal nature.

Marlowe also used orthodox witch theory for the conjuring scenes in the play. John Foxe's *Acts and Monuments,* or *Foxe's Book of Martyrs* was used by Marlowe as a source for the scenes treating Pope Adrian and the pretender to the papacy, Bruno.

**2. THE TEXT AND AUTHORSHIP:** It is difficult to establish exactly what constitutes the text of *Doctor Faustus,* but scholars tend to favor the 1616 version of the play over the 1604 quarto version. The term quarto refers to the page size of a printed book, and it means a book made of sheets which are folded into four leaves, or eight pages about nine by twelve inches in size. The 1604 quarto of *Doctor Faustus* runs to one thousand five hundred and seventeen lines and lacks the following episodes which are in the 1616 version: Bruno, the anti-pope; the revenge by the injured knight against Faustus; the horse-courser episode; and a number of the spectacular supernatural incidents of the last three scenes. These scenes in the 1616 version cause problems, too, for they seem to be included for no other purpose than farce and slapstick. They point to the fact that Marlowe was joined by another playwright, Samuel Rowley, in the composition of the play. As a play, *Doctor Faustus* was popular in its day, since it was acted many times between 1594 and 1597. Nine editions of *Doctor Faustus* we published from 1604 to 1631.

## 3. DRAMATIC TRADITIONS:

**a. THE MORALITY PLAY.** Together with the medieval mystery cycles, the morality play exerted a profound influence upon tht development of the English popular drama. Morality plays such as *Everyman* (14c.) presented the spiritual struggle for the soul of man waged by the forces of good and evil. The characters in the morality plays were personified abstractions, such as Everyman, Death, Good Fellowship, Good Deeds, Beauty, Strength. Allegory in the morality plays was the drama- tic means to present a didactic lesson which illustrated, as in *Everyman,* that only Good Deeds would go with man at the moment of death. Essentially the story of man's spiritual jour- ney, his combat against the adversaries of the world, the flesh, and the devil, and his spiritual salvation provided the core for morality drama. Man's antagonist or the Vice became a highly effective dramatic character because he was the villainous seducer of mankind. The influence of the morality Vice can be seen in such great characters as Falstaff in Shakespeare's *Henry IV, Part I,* where we see Falstaff, like the morality Vice, seducing Prince Hal from his princely responsibilities. Iago in *Othello* by his intrigue also reveals a definite link with the older type drama. The trend of the morality play in its later stages in the sixteenth century was to move away from the spiritual to more secular concerns and to present characters with greater individuality than the personified ab- stractions. Thus, such a play as Thomas Preston's *Cambises* (c. 1558-1570) is an important example of the transition from the more generalized morality play to a kind of historical tragedy which illustrated how a tyrant is rewarded with retri- butory punishment on earth, usually by physical death. It should also be said that *Cambises* is a curious blend of morality, farce, allegory, and tragedy. It is really a transitional type of hybrid drama between the morality and the popular plays of the 1580's and 1590's. To sum up, the morality play is an im- portant formative influence upon the themes and the structure of Elizabethan drama, and Marlowe's *Doctor Faustus* will re- veal many of these influences.

**b. TRAGEDY.**    During the Middle Ages the terms "tragedy" and "comedy" were applied to particular kinds of narrative and were not used in reference to an acted performance or drama. Basically the medieval conception of tragedy was that it was a narrative which illustrated the vagaries of fortune and the direful results to man of the Seven Deadly Sins, chief of which was Pride. Thus, by way of example, Chaucer's Monk, who tells a series of tragedies based on the lives of such men as Adam, Samson, and Caesar, gives a definition of tragedy in the *Prologue* to *The Monk's Tale* in *The Canterbury Tales*:

> Tragedie is to seyn a certeyn storie,
> As olde bookes maken us memorie,
> Of hym that stood in greet prosperitee,
> And is yfallen out of heigh degree
> Into myserie, and endeth wrecchedly.

Quite simply for the Monk tragedy is a story which narrates man's descent from good fortune to misery. Comedy, on the other hand, for the medieval period was a narrative which told of the ascent from bad fortune to good fortune; Dante's *Divine Comedy* with its movement from the *Inferno* to the *Paradiso* and the ultimate vision of joy is a fine example of what comedy meant in the Middle Ages. Also at the end of Chaucer's *Troilus and Criseyde,* Troilus speaks of his suffering and death as a tragedy, but when he ascends to the eighth sphere and to salvation in Christian terms, he refers to his story as a comedy. Importantly, then, it should be remembered that narrative and not drama for the medieval period illustrated the tragic and comic visions. Narrative also has a vital bearing on the growth of Elizabethan drama because plots were taken from narratives. Shakespeare, for instance, found the plots for his history plays in such narrative sources as *Holinshed's Chronicle.*

**DEVELOPMENT OF POPULAR DRAMA:**    The development of English popular drama from its origins in the medieval mystery and miracle plays until the time of Marlowe and Shakespeare is a long and quite complicated process. However, a few of the major influences should be mentioned in order that some of the forming influences might be seen. Of course, as we have seen, the morality play was a most important influence, and moralities continued to be acted until late into the sixteenth century. The morality play provided a native source and influence, and moralities continued to be acted until late into the sixteenth century. The morality play provided a native source and influence for the flourishing of Elizabethan drama. Along with native sources such as the morality play and the plays of professional troupes which travelled about England, we must consider the classical influence especially of Seneca, the Roman tragic dramatist, upon English tragedy. At the universities of Cambridge and Oxford, dramatists such as Thomas Kyd, Christopher Marlowe, John Lyly, and Robert Greene studied the classical dramatists Seneca, Plautus, and Terence. Seneca, a model text for the study of Rhetoric, was the chief classical influence upon the growth of Elizabethan tragedy. Though Seneca's dramas were never performed and were intended for oral reading ("closet drama"), their influence upon the Elizabethans was considerable. Plautus and Terence gave to Elizabethan drama its five act structure, and they were extremely influential forces upon the development of Elizabethan comedy. Stock figures such as the *miles gloriosus* (the braggart soldier), for example Falstaff in *Henry IV, Part I,* owe their origin to Roman Comedy. Also Shakespeare directly borrowed the plot and the farcical tone of his *The Comedy of Errors* from Plautus's *The Twin Menechmi.*

**INFLUENCE OF SENECA:**  Senecan tragedy, at any rate, gave to Elizabethan tragedy a ready example of the use of violence, horror, and revenge. The revenge plot became a staple ingredient of Elizabethan and Jacobean tragedy, and among its outstanding examples are Thomas Kyd's *The Spanish Tragedy* and Shakespeare's *Hamlet.* Seneca also influenced the style of Elizabethan tragedy because his bombastic rhetoric was carried over by his imitators, especially Kyd. The sensationalism, violence, and intrigue of Senecan tragedy are amply revealed in extreme form in Shakespeare's early play *Titus Andronicus.* Marlowe's *The Jew of Malta* also contains a good deal of the sensational violence and intrigue characteristic of Senecan revenge tragedy.

But the influence of Seneca was first felt in academic plays produced at the Inns of Court. Plays like *Gorboduc* (1561/ 1562), *Jocasta* (1566), *Gismond of Salerne* (1567/1568), and *The Misfortunes of Arthur* (1588) constitute prime examples of this type drama. All of these plays, with the exception of *Gismond,* deal with political problems, and they reveal how suffering and death are the just punishments for evil acts. *Gismond* treats the destructive nature of lust. The theme of these plays in a collective sense is the suffering and evil caused by the overthrow of reason by such destructive passions as ambition, lust, and the desire for revenge.

**ELIZABETHAN STAGE BENEFITS FROM NON-DRAMATIC LITER- ATURE:**     Elizabethan tragedy also has roots in non-dramatic literature such as *A Myrroure For Magistrates: Wherein may be seen by example of other, with howe greuous plages vices are punished: and howe frayle unstable worldly prosperitie is founde, euen of those, whom Fortune seemeth most highly to fauour.* The title of this work reveals its links with the works of Chaucer, Lydgate, and Boccaccio's *De Casibus Virorum Illustrium* (Of the Falls of Illustrious Men). The *Mirror for Magistrates* by its title reveals that it was a "mirror" wherein man might behold numerous examples testifying to the transience of worldly prosperity and the fickleness of fortune. The histories of men recounted in the *Mirror* and in the non-dramatic literature of the *de casibus* type provided the Elizabethan stage an abundance of stories to be dramatized and these stories also gave the dramatists an attitude toward the themes of mutability, suffering, evil, and death. Thus Sir Philip Sidney in his *Defense of Poesie* (1583) wrote the following about tragedy: ". . . of the high and excellent tragedy, that openeth the greatest wounds, and showeth forth ulcers that are covered with tissue, that maketh kings fear to be tyrants, and tyrants manifest their tyrannical humors, that with stirring the affects of admiration and commiseration teacheth the uncertainty of this world, and upon how weak foundations gilded roofs are builded. . . ."

**INFLUENCE OF KYD:**     The violence, revenge, horror, and sensationalism of Thomas Kyd's *The Spanish Tragedy* gave the English popular theater the basic conventions and attitudes that were to shape its tragic drama. Kyd, while showing the retributory nature of suffering, also focused upon the grim irony of tragedy that the innocent, too, are liable to suffering. Kyd's tragic universe revealed that villainous intrigue was in the end hoist on its own petard, but in the process villainy inflicted suffering and evil upon its victims. From Kyd the Elizabethan theater took the convention of revenge wherein the dilemma between a desire for true justice and the evil desire for blood and personal vengeance could be seen contending. Marlow then is the inheritor of the many streams that converge to make possible the growth of English drama. It is Marlowe's genius, however, that he can draw from the past and from contemporaries such as Kyd to shape a unique tragic conception.

# DETAILED SUMMARY OF
## *DOCTOR FAUSTUS*

### DRAMATIC CHARACTERS

**THE CHORUS:** introduces the action and serves to comment at the end of the play.

**DOCTOR FAUSTUS:** The learned professor who undertakes the study of magic.

**WAGNER:** Doctor Faustus's servant.

**VALDES:** ⎱ Both are friends of Faustus and know the
**CORNELIUS:** ⎰ secrets of magic.

**THREE SCHOLARS:** They are learned men of the University of Wittenberg.

**AN OLD MAN:** He offers advice to Faustus late in the play.

**THE POPE:** He is tricked by Faustus's magic.

**RAYMOND, KING OF HUNGARY:** Member of the Pope's party.

**BRUNO:** The anti-Pope who is rescued at Rome by Faustus.

**TWO CARDINALS:** ⎱ These figures appear at Rome when
**ARCHBISHOP OF RHEIMS:** ⎬ Faustus and Mephistophilis play
**CARDINAL OF LORRAINE:** ⎰ pranks against the Pope.

**CHARLES, EMPEROR OF GERMANY:** Entertains Faustus in gratitude for the help given to Bruno.

**MARTINO:**
**FREDERICK:** These three gentlemen of the court of Charles
**BENVOLIO:** are victims of Faustus's magic.

**DUKE OF ANHOLT:** Faustus shows him an enchanted castle in the air.

**CLOWN:** Taken into Wagner's service by magic.

**ROBIN:** A stableman who pursues magic.

**DICK:** An ally to Robin's conjuring.

**A HORSE-COURSER:** He is duped by Faustus into buying a horse which turns into a bundle of hay.

**HOSTESS:** Faustus strikes her dumb when she asks him to pay his bill at the tavern.

**GOOD ANGEL:** They advise Faustus and contend
**BAD ANGEL:** for his soul.

**MEPHISTOPHILIS:** A devil who assists Faustus.

**LUCIFER:** Prince of devils to whom Faustus sells his soul.

**BEELZEBUB:** A devil who is second to Lucifer in command.

**THE SEVEN DEADLY SINS:** Personifications of sins.

**ALEXANDER THE GREAT**
**HIS PARAMOUR**
**DARIUS** All of these are spirits who
**HELEN** are conjured up during the play.
**TWO CUPIDS**

**OTHER CHARACTERS: DUKE OF SAXONY, A KNIGHT, BISH-OPS, MONKS, FRIARS, SOLDIERS, EVIL ANGEL, RALPH, A VINTNER, A CARTER, DEVILS.**

## ACT I

Faustus sits in his study meditating on the various courses of study that he might pursue. Already he is a learned doctor of the University of Wittenberg, and now he rejects such traditional and orthodox studies as philosophy, law, medicine, and theology. Faustus desires to be free and human learning, he believes, is empty when compared to necromancy, or black magic. Although his Good Angel counsels Faustus to give up his plan to study necromancy Faustus persists in his design and heeds the urgings of the Bad Angel. Valdes and Cornelius, Faustus's friends, also urge him to pursue magic, and Faustus resolves that "This night I'll conjure, though I die therefore." Wagner, Faustus's servant, meets two scholars who are acquainted with Faustus, and when Wagner tells them that his master is dining with Valdes and Cornelius, the scholars express fear and rush off to tell the Rector of the University in the hope that there might yet be something that could be done to reclaim Faustus.

Faustus begins his magical career by conjuring up Mephistophilis from hell. Mephistophilis so frightens Faustus that he commands the demon to leave and to return dressed as a Franciscan friar. Mephistophilis does this and then answers Faustus's questions about hell and Lucifer. Faustus agrees to a bargain wherein he sells his soul to Lucifer for twenty-four years of voluptuous worldly pleasure with Mephistophilis for his servant.

The last scene of Act I presents a parody of the Faustus-Mephistophilis conjuring scene. Wagner, who has learned the ways of his master, tries to enlist a Clown in his service. When the Clown expresses reluctance, Wagner conjures two devils named Banio and Belcher who frighten the Clown to accept service.

## ACT II

Faustus again is seen sitting alone in his study, and he now thinks upon the significance of his bargain. His soul is in turmoil, and, though something seems to call him back from his damned course, Faustus proclaims his love for Beelzebub. The

Good and Evil Angels reappear to continue their contention for Faustus's soul. At the request of Mephistophilis, Faustus signs a contract with his own blood. When the blood congeals, Mephistophilis rushes out and brings in a chafer of fire to melt the blood so Faustus may continue to seal the bargain. To prevent Faustus from having any "second thoughts," Mephistophilis presents a show wherein devils present riches to Faustus, as a forecast of the pleasures that lie before him.

Faustus then reads the terms of the contract: he will surrender his soul to Lucifer after twenty-four years and during this time Mephistophilis is to assist Faustus and to do whatever he commands. After questioning Mephistophilis about hell, a wife is brought in and offered to Faustus, but Faustus rejects her and marriage. Mephistophilis promises to provide Faustus the "fairest courtesans" to satisfy his appetite. A book of instruction on how to practice magic is given to Faustus by Mephistophilis, and now the learned scholar is equipped with the means to begin his time of earthly pleasure.

Faustus, though, is tormented by pangs of conscience about his bargain, and he talks of repentance. The two angels reappear to increase thoughts of remorse and persistence in Faustus. He disputes with Mephistophilis about the constitution of the universe and other matters, but Faustus is unable to drive away the torment of his soul. Finally, Lucifer and Beelzebub enter to dissuade Faustus from any thought of Christ and repentance, and they offer Faustus a show wherein each of the Seven Deadly Sins presents itself to Faustus. He is so delighted by this vision of sensual pleasure that he swears never again to think of repenting, and Lucifer gives him a book of instruction on how to change shapes. Thus, the powers of evil have conquered thoughts of repentance.

Robin, the ostler or stableman, has gotten one of Doctor Faustus's conjuring books, and, in a comic scene which parodies the main plot, Robin announces his intention to practice knavery through magic. Robin refuses to walk horses any more, and together with Dick, a servant, he marches off to the tavern to see if magic can get them food and drink. Robin's mundane expectations for magical powers are in marked contrast to the grandiose hopes of Faustus.

## ACT III

A Prologue tells us that Faustus has flown through the heavens, surveyed the seacoasts of the world, and examined the kingdoms of the earth through the use of magic. He has now come to Rome, the Prologue informs us, to see the Pope and to take part in his feast. The first scene of Act III shows Faustus and Mephistophilis within the Pope's private chamber, and Faustus talks of the many places and wonders of the world that he has recently seen. Now at Rome, Faustus resolves to practice villainy against the Pope with the assistance of Mephistophilis. When the Pope enters, he ascends his seat by walking upon the back of his rival for the Papacy, Bruno, who is now a captive in chains. Faustus and Mephistophilis disguise themselves as cardinals and report to the Pope that the Council has decreed imprisonment for Bruno until such time as it is decided whether he shall live or die. Bruno, with the aid of Faustus and Mephistophilis, escapes to the refuge of the Emperor. Faustus and Mephistophilis become invisible and torment the Pope at his banquet by snatching dishes and cups from his hands and by striking him on the face.

Robin and Dick enter with a stolen goblet, and a vintner's boy pursues them. The boy catches up to them, but when he searches them, Robin and Dick pass the goblet back and forth. To satisfy the boy, Robin draws a circle and reads from the conjuring book to get the goblet back. As a result of the conjuring, Mephistophilis arrives from Constantinople and is furious because they brought him back for this nonsense. Mephistophilis swears he will transform them into an ape and a dog, and then he hurries back to Faustus at Constantinople.

## ACT IV

The Chorus, by way of Prologue, tells that Faustus returned home after travelling throughout the world. His fame in learning is so great that the Emperor Charles V now entertains him at court. When the act begins, two gentlemen of the court, named Martino and Frederick, discuss the Emperor's arrival, Bruno's presence and the arrival of Faustus. At the Emperor's court, Faustus summons up Alexander the Great and his paramour for the Emperor's pleasure. Faustus also punishes Benvolio, a gentleman of the court, for doubting his magical prowess by placing a pair of horns on his head. Faustus later removes Benvolio's horns, but Benvolio, together with Martino and Frederick, attempts to revenge himself against Faustus. Faustus, however, thwarts their revenge plot and consigns them to punishments. With the aid of Mephistophilis and other devils, Faustus also drives off a band of attacking soldiers. After the gentlemen of the court have undergone their punishments, they withdraw from the world to live in obscurity.

Faustus, in this act, also has to deal with a Horse-Courser to whom he sells a horse for forty dollars with the warning that the horse is not to be ridden into water. When the Horse-Courser rides the horse into water, it turns into a bundle of hay. Angered by this misfortune, the Horse-Courser demands that Faustus return his money, and when Faustus refuses, the Horse-Courser pulls off one of Faustus's legs. The Horse-Courser runs off with the happy feeling that he has been revenged, but this is merely another of Faustus's magical tricks. The Horse-Courser now tells his tale to Robin and Dick. Together the clowns go to see Faustus who strikes each of them dumb before they can tell what happened to them as a result of Faustus's use of magic. Faustus, meanwhile, receives the plaudits of the Duke and Duchess of Anholt for showing them an enchanted castle in the air and for providing grapes in the month of January.

## ACT V

Faustus has now enjoyed his years of pleasure and power, and his end is fast approaching. He wills his worldly goods to his servant Wagner, and then he feasts with the learned scholars who tell him that they have decided Helen of Troy was the most beautiful woman who ever lived. The scholars ask Faustus to summon up for their delight this beauty of antiquity. When Faustus does so, the scholars express their gratitude and leave. Grace, in the form of an Old Man, appears now for the last time to plead with Faustus to desist and leave his damned course. Faustus is about to recant and to call upon the mercy of his Savior, but Mephistophilis enters and presents a dagger to Faustus. Mephistophilis counsels despair, threatens Faustus, and finally prevails, for Faustus rejects the Old Man and asks forgiveness by swearing to reaffirm his contract with Lucifer. The final pleasure that Faustus seeks is that Helen of Troy might be his mistress; so Faustus commits the heinous sin of copulating with a demon. Thus, by this act Faustus rejects the possibility of repentance and mercy.

During the last hours of his life, Faustus is left alone to await the end of his bargain. Thoughts of Christ and repentance storm his brain. But the grip of Lucifer is complete fear and his old resolve makes Faustus aware of his sinful nature. Faustus wishes that he might dissolve into the elements, that he were not man but a beast, and that mountains would fall upon him to blot out the sunlight. He curses the parents that bore him, but all leads ultimately to his tragic doom. Faustus ends his life with a gasp of surrender to Mephistophilis and the devils who lead him to eternal damnation in hell.

# DETAILED SUMMARY OF *THE TRAGICAL HISTORY OF DOCTOR FAUSTUS*

## ACT I: PROLOGUE

The Chorus opens the play acting as prologue by giving a narrative of Faustus's birth, life, and present condition as a scholar surfeiting on "cursed necromancy." Necromancy means conjuring or summoning up spirits of the dead for the purposes of magic, and it is associated with what we today would call "black magic." In the prologue the Chorus introduces us to

Faustus's greatness by telling us that his chief pursuit is learning and that Faustus is different from the heroes commonly
met in stories:

> Not marching in the fields of Thrasimen,
> Where Mars did mate the warlike Carthagens;
> Nor sporting in the dalliance of love,
> In courts of kings, where state is over-turn'd;
> Nor in the pomp of proud audacious deeds,
> Intends our Muse to vaunt his heavenly verse.

Faustus was born of base stock, but went on to the university
at Wittenberg where he distinguished himself in learning and
received a doctor's degree in divinity.

> **COMMENT:** The Chorus serves to bring us the expo-
> sition of narrative materials necessary for our understand-
> ing of the play. The use of the chorus enables Marlowe
> to set the scene and to give us what we need to know as
> we meet Faustus, "this man that in his study sits." Note
> the foreshadowing of Faustus's tragic end:
>
> > Till swoln with cunning, of a self-conceit,
> > His waxen wings did mount above his reach,
> > And, melting, heavens conspir'd his over-throw . . .

The reference in these lines is to the story of Icarus, whose
waxen wings, made by his father Daedalus, melted when
he flew too close to the sun and caused him to fall to his
death in the sea. The myth is intimately related to Faustus
because, like Icarus, he too overreaches human bounds
and is destroyed in the attempt.

## ACT I: SCENE ONE

Faustus sits alone in his study and meditates in a long soliloquy
on the various courses of study: philosophy, medicine, law, and
divinity. Faustus rejects all these studies because he finds them
"illiberal", or "not-freeing." He desires freedom from the normal

restraints upon man. Necromancy is his new passion and he dedicates himself to its study. The Good Angel and the Bad Angel then enter to advise Faustus. The Good Angel pleads with Faustus not to follow his evil desires while the Bad Angel urges him on.

> **COMMENT:**      The Good and Bad Angels are allegorical personifications belonging to the morality play tradition. As in the morality play, they are active participants in a struggle for a man's soul; in this case they contend for the soul of Faustus. They represent in an exterior sense the interior struggle of Faustus between good and evil.

Valdes and Cornelius, friends of Faustus, encourage him in his resolve to pursue magic. Faustus concludes the scene by remarking, "This night I'll conjure, though I die therefore." The comment reveals his determination to risk eternal damnation so that he may have magical powers.

**SUMMARY:**      The opening scene follows the exposition of the Chorus on the background of Faustus and provides the introduction to the problem of the play: the conflict between Faustus's determination to pursue necromancy and the orthodox restrictions against such. In other words, Scene One introduces us to the central figure of the play, Faustus, and to the basic conflict in the play. The contest waged within Faustus's soul is between God and Satan. It also serves to do the following:

1. In the opening speech of Faustus, we can determine through his dismissal of philosophy, medicine, law and theology, the great learning of the man.

2. The opening speech of Faustus reveals his determination to pursue cursed necromancy and not his chiefest bliss—eternal life.

3. The Good and Bad Angel debate the problem with Faustus.

4. Valdes and Cornelius are companions of Faustus.

## ACT I: SCENE TWO

This short scene opens before Faustus's house. Two scholars meet Wagner, Faustus's servant, who argues with them when they ask where Faustus is. Wagner comically parodies the scholastic logic of the students in his replies, and then tells them Faustus is dining with Valdes and Cornelius. The scholars immediately express fear that Faustus has "fallen into that damned art/ for which they two are infamous through the world." The Scholars leave to tell the Rector of the University and hope that there is yet something they may do to save Faustus.

## ACT I: SCENE THREE

Faustus enters to conjure (to summon up a demon by magic) in a grove and utters in Latin an incantation which brings Mephistophilis from Hell. However, Faustus commands Mephistophilis to go and return in the shape of "an old Franciscan friar;/ That holy shape becomes a devil best." Mephistophilis leaves and Faustus is pleased to note the "virtue" (power, in the Latin sense *virtus, virtutis*) that he now possesses. Mephistophilis returns, now like a Franciscan friar, and asks Faustus what he wants him to do. Faustus commands Mephistophilis to do whatever he shall ask of him, and he then questions Mephistophilis about his master Lucifer and about hell.

**COMMENT:** In this scene we see the first result of Faustus's choice, which involves the deliberate rejection of God. The conjuring scene produces Mephistophilis who will serve Faustus in his satanic commitment. The appearance of Mephistophilis as a Franciscan Friar (a Roman Catholic religious order) no doubt appealed to an audience largely anti-Catholic in sentiment. Faustus's questions about Lucifer are important, for Lucifer was the prime example of "aspiring pride and insolence." Faustus, in his rejection of orthodoxy, parallels the pride of Lucifer, and when he asks Mephistophilis about hell he learns:

> Why this is hell, nor am I out of it:
> Think'st thou that I, that saw the face of God
> And tasted the eternal joys of Heaven,
> Am not tormented with ten thousand hells,
> In being deprived of everlasting bliss?

These lines are very important, for they indicate that hell is a spiritual condition rather than a physical place. Hell is the not-God, the deprivation of eternal life and beatific vision.

Faustus, who boasts that he is not afraid of damnation, advises Mephistophilis to learn "manly fortitude," and not to feel a sense of loss for joys he shall never gain. A bargain is then made by Faustus with Lucifer whereby Faustus will surrender his soul after spending twenty-four years in a life of voluptuousness with Mephistophilis attending him. More simply stated, Faustus trades in his soul for twenty-four years of sinful pleasure. Faustus excitedly speaks of his bargain and of the results he foresees:

> Had I as many souls as there be stars,
> I'd give them all for Mephistophilis.
> By him I'll be great Emperor of the world,
> And make a bridge through the moving air,
> To pass the ocean with a band of men . . .

**SUMMARY:**     Scene Three introduces Mephistophilis and also does the following:

1. We see (in this scene) Faustus practicing his "cursed necromancy" which brings Mephistophilis from hell.

2. We learn of Faustus's bargain to surrender his soul to Lucifer after a life of twenty-four years of pleasure.

3. Dramatically, the scene serves to excite our expectations about Faustus's future life. We see that he has made his bargain, and now we anxiously await its results.

## ACT I: SCENE FOUR

Wagner, Faustus's servant, comes upon a Clown in this scene and tries to enlist the Clown in his service. The Clown, im- poverished and hungry, is reluctant until Wagner summons two devils which frighten the Clown into immediate acceptance of service. The Clown asks Wagner to teach him this "con- juring occupation."

**COMMENT:** This short scene parodies the main plot of Faustus-Mephistophilis and their bargain. The tone of the scene is comic, and the verbal jesting and quibbling are to be taken humorously as a parody of Faustus's use of learning. Wagner's ability to conjure devils is in comic contrast to the serious spiritual problems posed by the main plot. No doubt, the audience relished the fun in- volved in this scene.

**SUMMARY:** Scene Four provides an instance of a common feature of Elizabethan drama, namely the mingling of the serious and comic. In *Doctor Faustus,* the comic sub-plot serves not only to entertain the audience with lively action and jests, but it also mirrors, on a different level, Faustus's career.

## ACT II: SCENE ONE

Faustus is seen in his study meditating upon the awful conse- quences of his bargain. Alone on stage, he delivers a soliloquy which reveals to the audience the inner turmoil of his soul. Despair, the ultimate sin for the Christian, leads Faustus for- ward on his road to eternal damnation; appetite and "Bel- zebub" have become Faustus's new gods. Though something sounds in his ear which seems to call him back from his damned course, Faustus is resolute in his love for Beelzebub, and he promises: "To him I'll build an altar and a church,/ And offer lukewarm blood of new-born babes."

**COMMENT:** Here Faustus parodies the establishment of the Christian church and the slaughter of the Innocents by Herod in his attempt to kill the Christ child. Faustus's inversion indicates the blasphemous nature of his choice. He will build an altar not to God, but to Beelzebub, a demon second only to Satan in power. Again, too, we find in this soliloquy the repetition of the basic problem of the play: Faustus's choice of God or the not-God. His tragic struggle is essentially a contest between traditional orthodoxy and its antithesis, represented by Satan and his powers. It is important to note how this basic conflict is repeated throughout the play, for it embodies the moral contest between good and evil which is at the heart of Faustus's tragic dilemma.

Two Angels enter on the stage. The Good Angel advises Faustus to leave "that execrable art" and to think of heaven. The Bad Angel tells Faustus that contrition, prayer, and repentance are illusions that produce madness. The Bad Angel suggests instead that Faustus think of wealth, and with this Faustus calls up Mephistophilis. Mephistophilis now asks Faustus to seal the bargain and tells him that Lucifer pursues men simply because "Misery loves company." This reminds us of Satan in Milton's *Paradise Lost,* who in defeat resolves to war eternally against man, God's creature, through guile. Faustus stabs his arm and seals the bargain with his own blood. As he signs the contract, his blood congeals, and Mephistophilis rushes out to get a chafer of fire to melt the blood. Mephistophilis returns, the fire melts the blood, and the deal is concluded. Faustus, however, notices something written on his arm:

> *Homo, fuge!* Whither should I fly?
> If unto God, he'll throw me down to hell.
> My senses are deceiv'd; here's nothing writ:
> O yes, I see it plain; even here is writ,
> *Homo, fuge!* Yet shall not Faustus fly.

**COMMENT:** Again we see Faustus hovering between two extremes of choice, and when he seals the bargain with his blood note how the blood thickens briefly until Mephistophilis brings the chafer of fire to melt the blood. Suspense is created as we wonder whether Faustus will go through with his awful choice. The blood, the fire, and the devils certainly make for effective theater. When Faustus says *"Consummatum est"* ("It is finished"), he uses the last words of Christ on the Cross. With this blasphemous analogy to Christ, Faustus sells his soul to Lucifer. Faustus, too, would be a god.

To please Faustus, Mephistophilis presents a "dumb-show," a silent acting out of a meaningful situation, of devils presenting crowns and rich apparel to Faustus. Pleased by what he has seen and by the promise of magical powers, Faustus reads the conditions of his contract with Lucifer. The conditions are that Faustus will surrender "body and soul, flesh, blood" to Lucifer in exchange for twenty-four years of worldly pleasure and magical power. Mephistophilis is to assist Faustus during this period and is to do whatever Faustus commands. Faustus then asks Mephistophilis, "Where is the place that men call hell?" Mephistophilis replies:

> Hell hath no limits, nor is circumscrib'd
> In one self place; but where we are is hell,
> And where hell is, there must we ever be:
> And, to be short, when all the world dissolves,
> And every creature shall be purified,
> All places shall be hell that is not heaven.

Faustus refuses to believe that after this life there is pain, and he asks Mephistophilis for a wife. A woman-devil is fetched in by Mephistophilis. Faustus rejects the idea of marriage; Mephistophilis calls it a "ceremonial toy" and promises Faustus the "fairest courtesans." A book of instruction in magic is then given to Faustus by Mephistophilis.

**COMMENT:**    Mephistophilis's lines on hell are important, for they reveal to us that hell is a spiritual condition, the state of not being one with God. Contained in these lines is the description of Faustus's ultimate "reward" for entering into his contract with Lucifer. The "dumb-show", the appearance of the woman-devil, and the presentation of the book on magic are all part of the world of magical promise and power for which Faustus is willing to damn himself. Marlowe, in this scene, very effectively creates the atmosphere and mood of the supernatural and the magical.

**SUMMARY:**      This scene, in terms of the dramatic action, really begins the "action" as such because in it Faustus signs the contract with Lucifer for his soul. Act I was concerned with exposition, that is with acquainting the audience with the information needed to understand the subsequent action. Stated simply, it introduced us to Faustus, his temptation, and to Mephistophilis. Now in Act II, Scene I we see Faustus making his choice, and we look forward with anticipation to the results of his choice. Much of the rest of the play is concerned with illustrating or showing dramatically what it means and what happens as a result of Faustus's contract. Also this scene presents us with Faustus's inward doubt, his wavering in his commitment. The Good Angel embodies the call to repentance which strikes Faustus's conscience. The following points are also important:

1. Faustus indicates his rejection of God through his inverted use of traditional religious ritual and language. For instance, recall in this scene his shedding of blood to seal the contract and Faustus's parallel of this to Christ's shedding of blood in the Crucifixion. As Christ contracted to redeem man by the shedding of divine blood, so Faustus contracts to sell his soul to Lucifer and thereby to reject Christ.

2. The Good and Bad Angels reappear in this scene as external dramatic embodiments of Faustus's interior struggle.

3. The "dumb-show" is dramatically illustrative of what Faustus will gain through the contract. The promise of worldly wealth and power wins Faustus and he rejects the possibility of hell and pain as mere superstition.

## ACT II: SCENE TWO

The scene opens wtth Faustus and Mephistophilis alone on stage. Faustus talks of heaven. "I will renounce this magic and repent." The two angels enter again and plead with Faustus. The angels exit, and Faustus speaks of how it is impossible for him to repent. The temptation to despair and suicide has been conquered by the "sweet pleasure" which Faustus has gained from his new magical powers:

> Have I not made blind Homer sing to me
> Of Alexander's love and Oenon's death?
> And hath not he, that built the walls of Thebes,
> With ravishing sound of his melodious harp,
> Made music with my Mephistophilis?
> Why should I die, then or basely despair?
> I am resolv'd; Faustus shall not repent.

Faustus questions Mephistophilis about the constitution of the universe and asks who made the world. When Mephistophilis refuses to answer the question, Faustus again thinks of God, and the two angels reappear to urge their respective sides of the argument. Faustus cries out: "O, Christ, my Saviour, my Saviour,/Help to save distressed Faustus' soul!" At this point, Mephistophilis enters with Lucifer and Beelzebub who remind Faustus of his bargain and they warn him not to injure them by thinking on Christ. Faustus repents and promises nevermore ". . . to name God, or to pray to him,/ To burn his Scriptures, slay his ministers,/ And make my spirits pull his churches down." The Seven Deadly Sins appear to entertain Faustus and to divert his attention away from any thoughts of God and true repentance.

> **COMMENT:** The repetitive pattern of the struggle within Faustus' soul is seen at this point, for Faustus thinks of repentance. However, evil overcomes such thoughts, and we see that the appearance of Lucifer is important because he is needed to prevent Faustus from breaking the bargain. Faustus, recalled by Lucifer from repentance, promises

to make active war against God and his churches. This indicates that Faustus is an atheist, one who is actively anti-God.

The appearance of the Seven Deadly Sins (Pride, Covetousness, Envy, Wrath, Gluttony, Sloth, Lechery) is used to please Faustus and to renew his firmness in the bargain. The Seven Deadly Sins, so called because they are the chief enemies of the soul, frequently appeared in Medieval literature, particularly morality plays. In the morality play the central issue was the struggle between virtue and vice (the deadly sins) for man's soul. Here the Seven Deadly Sins reveal what Faustus is committing himself to—a life of moral abandon.

Each of the Seven Deadly Sins speaks of its peculiar nature, and they then exit. Faustus says: "O, how this sight doth delight my soul!" Lucifer gives Faustus a book which will instruct him how to change shapes. Thus the scene ends.

**SUMMARY:** This scene does the following:

1. It again shows the struggle in Faustus between good and evil.

2. The appearance of Lucifer and the Seven Deadly Sins prevents Faustus from repenting and turning to God.

3. With the appearance of the Seven Deadly Sins we are reminded of the older morality drama to which *Doctor Faustus* owes a great deal.

## ACT II: SCENE THREE

Robin, the ostler or stableman, has gotten one of Doctor Faustus's conjuring books and he refuses to walk the horses because he intends to practice knavery with the book. Dick joins Robin as they head for the tavern to see if magic will get them food and drink.

**COMMENT:** This scene is part of the comic sub-plot which parallels the action of the main plot. The farcical conjuring of Robin and Dick provides a commentary on the conjuring of the main plot in that it points up by contrast the serious nature of Faustus's bargain, which ironically is an empty one when juxtaposed with the consequence of eternal damnation.

## ACT III: PROLOGUE

The Prologue provides a body of narrative material concerning what Faustus does with his magical powers. To prove "the secrets of astronomy," Faustus has flown through the heavens, and "to prove cosmography" he has surveyed the coasts and kingdoms of the earth. Finally, Faustus comes to Rome to see the Pope and to take part in "Peter's feast."

**COMMENT:** Dramatically, the Prologue provides narrative material which it would have been difficult for Marlowe to present on stage. An important idea to retain when thinking of the structure of *Doctor Faustus* is that Marlowe was limited in what he could do to illustrate the magical powers of Faustus. Thus, as any dramatist is, Marlowe was limited by the physical possibilities of his artistic medium—the stage. The Elizabethan stage was, by our standards, rather limited in technical and scenic effects; however, some scenery was used. Usually a distinction is made in dramatic vocabulary by describing the Elizabethan stage as a theater of convention, one dependent upon agreement between the audience and playwright on ways of doing things. Thus, by way of example, the Prologue is a "conventional" way of relating narrative information, a tapestry hanging at the back of the stage suggests that the scene occurs in a court, and an actor entering from one side of the stage and exiting from the other side indicates to the audience that he is on a journey. Our theater today is normally a theater of illusion because it deliberately attempts to make the action and scene seem "true-to-life." The picture frame stage enclosing a living-room set is the most obvious example.

In the Prologue, notice also that Marlowe uses the Ptolemaic conception of the universe with the earth central and surrounded by nine spheres. The planets were located in each sphere and the outermost sphere was the *Primum Mobile,* beyond which was heaven. The spheres rotated and created thereby a celestial harmony not heard by man since the fall of Adam. The general conception of the universe described here was a commonplace in Elizabethan poetry.

## ACT III: SCENE ONE

Faustus and Mephistophilis are within the Pope's Privy chamber, and Faustus speaks of the many places that he has recently visited: Trier, Paris, Naples, Venice, Padua, and the East. He asks Mephistophilis if he is now at Rome. Mephistophilis assures him that he is, and he gives Faustus a description of Rome, "this city stands upon seven hills. . . ." Faustus, swearing by the infernal powers of Styx, Acheron, and Phlegethon, expresses the wish that he would like to see the sights of Rome. Mephistophilis, however, stays him and tells him to remain to participate in the Pope's feast. Faustus replies:

> Sweet Mephistophilis, thou pleasest me,
> Whilst I am here on earth, let me be cloy'd
> With all things that delight the heart of man.
> My four-and-twenty years of liberty
> I'll spend in pleasure and in dalliance,
> That Faustus' name, whilst this bright frame doth stand,
> May be admired through the furthest land.

Mephistophilis, now, after allowing Faustus to view the heavens for eight days, promises to aid Faustus in practicing villainy against the Pope, Cardinals, and Friars. The Pope enters in procession with Raymond, King of Hungary, and Bruno in chains. The Pope ascends Saint Peter's chair by stepping upon Bruno's back, and the Pope asserts that this is his vengeance. The Cardinals of France are then sent by the Pope to learn the findings of the Council of Trent concerning Bruno's attempt to occupy the Papal throne "without election, and a true consent."

**COMMENT:**     Again by means of narrative Marlowe relates the deeds accomplished by Faustus through magic and the aid of Mephistophilis. Mephistophilis emphasizes the idea of rejection of God by his invocation of hell to make Faustus invisible, and Faustus reiterates his commitment by addressing words of love and devotion to Mephistophilis and by calling him "sweet." Faustus desires to be "cloyed" (to be surfeited) by the pleasures of this world so that he may gain earthly fame.

Marlowe's account of Pope Adrian's victory over his rival Bruno and Adrian's treatment of the captive Bruno seems to be taken from John Foxe's *Acts and Monuments,* also known as *Foxe's Book of Martyrs.* Certain ecclesiastical terms that occur in this scene with their meanings are: "Consistory"—Papal meeting place or senate; "Statutes decretal"—ecclesiastical law, the decree of councils; "Schism"—a difference of opinion with regard to doctrine causing a split from a church.

Faustus asks Mephistophilis to follow the Cardinals and to "Strike them with sloth and drowsy idleness" because he wants Mephistophilis and himself to assume their places in parley with the Pope, "this proud confronter of the Emperor":

And in despite of all his Holiness.
Restore this Bruno to his liberty,
And bear him to the State of Germany.

Bruno, claiming election by the Emperor, disputes Pope Adrian on his right to the Papacy. Adrian says that he will excommunicate (separate from membership in the Church by depriving a person of the sacraments and other privileges) the proud Emperor for his haughty act:

> We will depose the Emperor for that deed,
> And curse the people that submit to him;
> Both he and thou shalt stand excommunicate,
> And interdict from Church's privilege
> And all society of holy men:
> He grows too proud in his authority,
> Lifting his lofty head above the clouds,
> And like a steeple over-peers the Church:
> But we'll pull down his haughty insolence.

**COMMENT:** The material concerning the Pope and the Emperor provides an historical analogy to the pride of Faustus in accepting temporal power at the price of spiritual damnation. The historical contention concerning Papal election brought into opposition the spiritual power of the Pope and Cardinals and the temporal power of the Emperor. Pope Adrian, in defense of his position, cites the historical example of his predecessor Pope Alexander III (1159-1181) who forced the Emperor Frederick Barbarossa to acknowledge Papal supremacy. Thus, too, early in 1570 Pius V issued a Papal Bull excommunicating Queen Elizabeth. This denied her right to the throne and forbade her subjects to obey her:

> So we will quell that haughty schismatic;
> And by authority apostolical
> Depose him from his regal government.

Bruno states that Pope Julius swore that the German Emperor Sigismund was his princely lord and that succeeding popes should do likewise. However, Pope Adrian claims that Pope Julius abused his office and that none of his decrees therefore were binding. The Pope then points to the seven golden keys which betoken the sevenfold power granted him from heaven.

**COMMENT:** There was no Pope Julius during the lifetime of the German Emperor Sigismund (1368-1437), and thus Marlowe uses fiction here. The keys which the Pope points to are the traditional keys of Saint Peter, the first Pope, and they also symbolize the power of the seven sacraments.

Faustus and Mephistophilis enter disguised as Cardinals, and the Pope asks them to report the results of the Consistory concerning Bruno and the Emperor. Faustus reports that by unanimous consent it was decreed:

> That Bruno and the German Emperor
> Be held as Lollards and bold schismatics
> And proud disturbers of the Church's peace.

The Pope then orders Bruno imprisoned until it is determined whether he shall live or die, and Faustus and Mephistophilis exit leading Bruno to prison. The Pope concludes the scene on a note of joy:

> Go presently and bring a banquet forth,
> That we may solemnize Saint Peter's feast,
> And with Lord Raymond, King of Hungary,
> Drink to our late and happy victory.

**COMMENT:** The use of disguise by Faustus enables him to deceive the Pope and establishes an ironic contrast between the outward garment of the religious office and the true nature of Faustus and his evil bargain. Though much of what Faustus does in this scene is farce, yet there is some seriousness because the action illustrates Faustus's war against God and his churches. Undoubtedly an Elizabethan audience enjoyed the spectacle of the Pope's deception since anti-Catholic sentiment was strong at the time in England. But it is not too far-fetched to say that the audience would have recognized here Faustus practicing his atheism.

**SUMMARY:** Act III, Scene One does the following:

1. It shows the powers Faustus has achieved by selling his soul. From a structural and dramatic point of view, Marlowe's use of narrative technique to illustrate these powers and accomplishments is important.

2. This scene also begins the dramatic portions of the play which are chiefly comic and which may well have been written by Samuel Rowley.

## ACT III: SCENE TWO

A banquet is brought in, and Faustus and Mephistophilis appear now in their own shapes. Mephistophilis reports that Bruno has escaped "to salute the woeful Emperor." Faustus asks Mephistophilis to make him invisible so that he may go about the banquet unseen. Mephistophilis, invoking hell and and Furies, complies with the request. The Pope enters the banquet with the Lords, and the Cardinals enter with a book. The Cardinals ask the Pope if he wishes to hear the sentence of the Consistory concerning Bruno, but the Pope recalls that they had already reported their findings to him. Of course, the Pope has been deceived and is now confronted by the real Consistory, and he cries out for foul punishment on the false prelates who deceived him. The banquet proceeds and Faustus, now invisible, plays pranks on the Pope by snatching away his dish and cup. When the Pope crosses himself to ward off the spirit, Faustus strikes him, and the Pope cries out:

> O I am slain, help me, my lords;
> O come and help to bear my body hence:——
> Damn'd be his soul for ever for this deed!

Mephistophilis warns Faustus that now he will be cursed "with bell, book, and candle," which refers to a form of excommunication wherein at the end the bell is tolled, the book is closed, and the candle is blown out. Then the Friars sing "Maledicat Dominus"—a curse upon the Pope's enemies.

**SUMMARY:**　　Scene Two of Act III presents Faustus as a practical joker who heckles the Pope. The diminution of the stature of Faustus here may be attributable to the hand of a collaborator insufficiently attuned to the grand scale of Marlowe's tragic design. Perhaps, though, this scene should be viewed as comic and ironic too, for it points out clearly the awful chasm which separates Faustus's bargain for worldly pleasure from eternal salvation.

## ACT III: SCENE THREE

Robin and Dick enter with a stolen goblet, and they are pursued by the vintner's boy. When the vintner's boy catches up with them, he searches them, but Robin and Dick pass the goblet from one to the other. Robin orders Dick to make a circle, and he reads from his conjuring book to get the goblet back. Dick's conjuring summons Mephistophilis from Constantinople, but Mephistophilis in anger swears he will transform them into an ape and a dog for their foolery. The Clowns exit, and Mephistophilis returns to Faustus at the Great Turk's Court.

**SUMMARY:**　　The comic sub-plot here reminds us of the comedy in Act II, Scene Three. Again the conjuring of Robin and Dick is a parody of the serious action of the main plot.

## ACT IV—PROLOGUE

The Chorus narrates that when Faustus had travelled about the world and had been filled with pleasure, he returned home to demonstrate his skill and learning by answering questions in astrology. Faustus's fame has now spread throughout the world, and he is entertained by the Emperor Charles V. The Chorus remarks about this incident:

> What there he did, in trial of his art,
> I leave untold; your eyes shall see perform'd.

## ACT IV: SCENE ONE

Martino and Frederick, gentlemen of the Court of Charles V, enter and discuss preparations for the arrival of the Emperor. Martino says that Bruno will attend the Emperor, and that with him comes the famous German conjurer, Faustus.

> The learned Faustus, fame of Wittenberg,
> The wonder of the woild for magic art;
> And he intends to show great Carolus
> The race of all his stout progenitors;
> And bring in presence of his Majesty
> The royal shapes and warlike semblances
> Of Alexander and his beauteous paramour.

Martino and Frederick then call Benvolio, their fellow gentleman of the court, who has slept late because he drank too much the night before in celebration of Bruno's return. They summon Benvolio to court to see the performance of marvellous exploits by Faustus, but Benvolio tells them to go without him. He explains: "I have a charm in my head shall control him as well as the conjurer, I warrant you."

**SUMMARY:**     This scene provides the exposition necessary to change the scene from Rome to the Court of the Emperor. The minor characters in dialogue give us the setting, what has happened, and what we may expect in the next scene. The scene, in general, is an introduction to Faustus's career at the Court of Emperor Charles V.

## ACT IV: SCENE TWO

The scene opens in the presence chamber of the Emperor who hails Faustus for freeing Bruno and promises Faustus that he shall be famous if Bruno succeeds to the "triple diadem" (Pope's crown). Faustus states that he will put his powers to the service of the Emperor. Meanwhile Benvolio has been watching this from his window above and in an aside expresses doubt that Faustus is a conjuror. The Emperor asks Faustus to conjure Alexander the Great and his paramour so that they "may wonder at their excellence." Faustus says that he will do so, but he demands that the Emperor ask no questions of Alexander and Roxana, his wife. Benvolio continues his expression of doubt concerning Faustus's powers, and Faustus warns Benvolio that he will turn him into a stag with horns. Here Faustus refers to the myth of Diana and her nymphs, who while bathing were interrupted by Acteon who was punished for his spying by being changed into a stag by the goddess. Acteon's own dogs then tore him to pieces.

A "dumb show" is then presented in which the Emperor Alexander and Darius enter at opposite doors; they fight, and Alexander kills Darius, takes his crown, and places the crown on his paramour's head. Alexander and his paramour then salute the Emperor, who is so ravished by the sight that he goes forward to embrace them. But Faustus prevents him, and the sight of a mole on the neck of Alexander's paramour proves the truth of the scene to the Emperor.

> **COMMENT:**    The "dumb-show" is a silent show wherein recognizable characters or allegorical personifications act out a meaningful situation. Perhaps a modern pantomime might suggest more clearly what it is. At any rate, the dumb-show was frequently used in Elizabethan drama, especially Senecan-type dramas; *Gorboduc, The Spanish Tragedy,* and *Hamlet* are outstanding examples. In *Hamlet,* for instance, the "play-within-a play" contains many of the same features: *The Murder of Gonzago* when acted presses home the analogy of its action to the murder of Hamlet's father by Claudius. Here in *Dr. Faustus* the dumb-show is a dramatic device which enables Marlowe to show the magical powers of Faustus. Also the action of the show is a comment by way of analogy upon the career of Emperor Charles V, whose ambition and pride aspire to rival that of Alexander the Great. Faustus's pride is also involved, for his basic sin is that of presumption and pride.

The Emperor looks up and notices Benvolio asleep in the

window with a pair of horns on his head which prevent him from pulling his head back through the window. Benvolio asks Faustus if this is his villainy. Faustus, recalling Benvolio's questioning of his powers, warns Benvolio that he will now "raise a kennel of hounds" to hunt him. Benvolio pleads forgiveness from Faustus, and the Emperor aids him by asking Faustus to remove the horns. Faustus then commands Mephistophilis to remove Benvolio's horns, and the scene ends with Benvolio swearing revenge for his humiliation.

> **COMMENT:**     This episode with Benvolio presents a comic and farcical illustration of Faustus's magical powers. It contrasts sharply with the preceding "serious" display of magic in the conjuring of Alexander and his paramour. The tone of this scene is really one with the comic subplot treating Wagner, Robin, and Dick. Also, in terms of the overall meaning of the play, this scene is meant to reveal the absurdity of Faustus's bargain through the startling contrast of his dream of greatness and the horrifying reality that his power makes him a practical joker.

**SUMMARY:**     Act IV, Scene Two is important because:

1. It continues the dramatic illustration of Faustus's magical career. Faustus conjures Alexander and his paramour to delight the Emperor.

2. The dumb-show, as used in the Elizabethan era, was a conventional dramatic device to convey a certain meaning, and in this scene Marlowe employs it to present the career of Alexander, which parallels the ambitious career of the Emperor Charles V. Also, this *exemplum,* or moral commentary, provides a lesson on pride because the Emperor indicates his desire to be like Alexander. We may further note that Faustus, too, is guilty of pride in his rejection of God for "cursed necromancy" and worldly power.

3. The Benvolio episode is a comic contrast to the "serious" major action and presents the farcical side of Faustus's bargain.

## ACT IV: SCENE THREE

Benvolio persuades Martino and Frederick to assist him in an attempt to avenge his injury against Faustus:

> O may these eyelids never close again,
> Till with my sword I have that conjuror slain.
> If you will aid me in this enterprise,
> Then draw your weapons, and be resolute:
> If not, depart: here will Benvolio die,
> But Faustus' death shall quit my infamy.

Frederick and Martino promise to assist Benvolio, and they hide to await the entrance of Faustus. Benvolio hopes to have Faustus's head in exchange for the horns which Faustus placed upon his head. Faustus enters wearing a false head. Benvolio stabs him and strikes off his false head. Frederick suggests that they devise more shame to place on Faustus's hated name, and Benvolio says:

> First, on his head, in quittance of my wrongs,
> I'll nail huge forked horns, and let them hang
> Within the window where he yok'd me first,
> That all the world may see my just revenge.

Benvolio further plans to sell Faustus's head to a chimney-sweeper and to make his eyes buttons "to keep his tongue from catching cold." At this point Faustus rises from the ground and strikes terror into Benvolio, Martino, and Frederick. Faustus tells them that their efforts to kill him were useless because his bargain calls for twenty-four years of life, and then summons Mephistophilis and other devils to exact revenge:

> Go, horse these traitors on your fiery backs,
> And mount aloft with them as high as heaven,
> Thence pitch them headlong to the lowest hell:
> Yet, stay, the world shall see their misery,
> And hell shall after plague their treachery.

Punishments are then meted out: one is to be hurled into a lake, the second is to be dragged through thorny woods, and Benvolio is to be thrown from a cliff so that his bones are broken. Some soldiers enter to ambush Faustus, but he defeats them with the aid of Mephistophilis and other devils.

**SUMMARY:**     In this scene we see continued the farcical side of Faustus's career as magician. The abortive revenge plot of Benvolio undoubtedly was quite successful theater with its cuckold's horns, ambush, and battle between soldiers and devils. The appearance of Mephistophilis in the battle with fireworks also served to make for exciting moments in the theater. In terms of the relationship of the scene to the overall meaning and structure of the play, it should be viewed as another farcical episode and one more ironic illustration of the bargain of Faustus with Lucifer. Also we see in this scene the comic use of a stock theme of serious Elizabethan tragedy, namely revenge. Benvolio's revenge plot against Faustus is thwarted by magic of a comic order.

### ACT IV: SCENE FOUR

Benvolio, Frederick, and Martino enter, and their heads and faces are bloody from their punishments. They all have cuckold's horns on their heads, and they discuss their mutual shame. Benvolio proposes that they withdraw to live obscurely and to hide their disgrace:

> I have a castle joining near these woods,
> And thither we'll repair and live obscure,
> Till time shall alter these our brutish shapes:
> Sith black disgrace hath thus eclips'd our fame,
> We'll rather die with grief than live with shame.

### ACT IV: SCENE FIVE

In this episode Faustus deals with a Horse-Courser, or horse-dealer, who as a group had a notorious reputation for dishonesty. Faustus sells a horse to the Horse-Courser and warns him not to ride the horse into water. The Horse-Courser leaves, and Faustus delivers a soliloquy in which he contemplates the final end of his bargain:

> What art thou, Faustus, but a man condemn'd to die?
> Thy fatal time draws to a final end,
> Despair doth drive distrust into my thoughts.
> Confound these passions with a quiet sleep.
> Tush! Christ did call the thief upon the Cross;
> Then rest thee, Faustus, quiet in conceit.

**COMMENT:**    In this soliloquy, Faustus dramatically reminds us of his approaching end and interrupts the comic action to provide serious reflection on his destiny. When Faustus reminds himself that he is destined "to die," we know that his death is not merely physical, but it also involves spiritual destruction. His "fatal time," that time allowed by fate, is now fast approaching its close, and troublesome thoughts intrude upon Faustus's worldly pleasure. Presumptuously, he thinks of the thief on the cross whom Christ forgave; however, implicitly we are aware, too, of the other thief on the cross who failed to call upon Christ for mercy and forgiveness. Faustus finally dispels these disturbing thoughts by returning to the quiet of imaginative dreams and longings for the pleasures of appetite. Once again pride and presumption are victorious over thoughts of repentance.

The Horse-Courser enters and he is literally soaking wet from a disastrous horse ride. He demands that Faustus return his money, and in a scuffle with Faustus over the money, the Horse-Courser pulls off one of Faustus's legs. The Horse-Courser runs and thinks that he can outrun Faustus who now has only one leg; however, Faustus laughs with great joy because he has deceived the Horse-Courser into buying a horse which really was nothing but a bundle of hay. Faustus has swindled the Horse-Courser out of forty dollars. Wagner, Faustus's servant, enters and tells his master that the Duke of Anholt desires his company.

**SUMMARY:**    In this scene we see the following:

1. Faustus tricking the Horse-Courser.

2. Faustus pausing to think of his approaching end—his "fatal time." His soliloquy foreshadows the final hours of his life.

## ACT IV: SCENE SIX

Robin, Dick, the Horse-Courser, and a Carter are in an inn talking bawdily about their bills for drink and about women. The Carter tells a tale about how Faustus gave him three farthings for as much hay as he could eat. Faustus thereupon ate the Carter's entire load of hay. The Horse-Courser in turn narrates his tale concerning the horse who turned into a "bottle of hay," when he rode into water. However, the Horse-Courser joyfully tells all that he has been revenged, for Faustus now has but one leg. Dick expresses his happiness at this news because Faustus had turned his face into the likeness of an ape. Robin proposes that they drink for a while and that they then should go to see the fabulous Doctor.

## ACT IV: SCENE SEVEN

This scene occurs at the Court of the Duke of Anholt, who opens the scene by expressing thanks to Faustus for having shown him the pleasing sight of an enchanted castle in the air. Faustus asks the Duchess: "What is the thing you most desire to have; be it in the world, it shall be yours." She asks for a dish of grapes even though the month is January. Mephistophilis is commanded to fetch the grapes, and he returns quickly with grapes obtained in India.

The clowns are heard knocking loudly at the gates, and they cry out that they want to speak to Faustus. When they enter, Faustus greets them and tells them that he has procured their pardons. The clowns create an uproar and demand beer. Faustus tells them they shall have beer, and the Horse-Courser says: "I'll drink a health to thy wooden leg for that word." Faustus pretends not to understand what the Horse-Courser is talking about and shows the clowns that he has both legs. They scream: "O horrible, had the Doctor three legs?" Each of them asks Faustus if he remembers the tricks played upon them, but before they can finish their questions, Faustus strikes them dumb. The Hostess, too, is struck dumb by Faustus when she asks who shall pay the bill for the beer. The Duke and the Duchess of Anholt conclude the scene by expressing gratitude for Faustus's "artful sport" which "drives all sad thoughts away."

**SUMMARY:** Act IV, Scene Seven concludes the fourth act of *Doctor Faustus* and brings to an end the farcical episodes illustrating Faustus's magical powers. Throughout the act, in a series of episodic actions which are structurally related because each repeats basically the pattern of dramatic illustration of what it means to reject God, Faustus is presented as a practical joker. Much of this act, the last scene for example, certainly made for good theater because the audience relished the magic, fireworks, and the pranks. One thing that Elizabethan revenge tragedy reveals is that Elizabethan audiences had a special fondness for sensationalism, horror, and blood. However, with regard to serious meaning, the fourth act ironically reveals the limitations of Faustus's bargain; we ask: "Is this worth the price of eternal damnation?" Faustus's powers are certainly meager. Indeed, at times they are ludicrous, as we see in the comic action of Scene Seven, which treats the gulling of the clowns.

### ACT V: SCENE ONE

The scene opens with thunder and lightning, and devils carry in covered dishes. Mephistophilis leads the devils into Faustus's study. Wagner enters, and after Faustus wills him his wealth, Wagner is convinced that the great Doctor is about to die. Faustus now feasts with the scholars, and the First Scholar

tells Faustus that the scholars have decided that Helen of
Greece was the fairest woman who ever lived and that they
now wish Faustus to make it possible for them to see her. Faustus assures the scholars that he will grant their request, and
Mephistophilis brings in Helen and she passes across the stage.
The three scholars all agree that they have witnessed an extraordinary sight, and they express gratitude to Faustus.

An Old Man enters and counsels Faustus:

> O gentle Faustus, leave this damned art,
> This magic, that will charm thy soul to hell,
> And quite bereave thee of salvation.
> Though thou hast now offended like a man,
> Do not persever in it like a devil;
> If sin by custom grow not into nature:
> Then, Faustus, will repentance come too late,
> Then thou art banish'd from the sight of heaven;
> No mortal can express the pains of hell.

The Old Man exhorts Faustus to do as he advises so that he
may amend his soul while there is time. Faustus replies to the
advice of the Old Man:

> Break heart, drop blood, and mingle it with tears,
> Tears falling from repentant heaviness
> Of thy most vile and loathsome filthiness,
> The stench whereof corrupts the inward soul
> With such flagitious crimes of heinous sins
> And no commiseration may expel,
> But mercy, Faustus, of thy Saviour sweet,
> Whose blood alone must wash away thy guilt—
> Where art thou, Faustus? Wretch, what hast thou done?
> Damn'd art thou, Faustus, Damn'd; despair and die!

Mephistophilis gives Faustus a dagger, and Faustus says:

> Hell claims his right, and with a roaring voice
> Says, 'Faustus, come; thine hour is almost come';
> And Faustus now will come to do thee right.

The Old Man pleads with Faustus to acknowledge the angel of grace which hovers over his head and to avoid despair. Now Faustus asks the Old Man to leave him for a time so that he may ponder on his sins. The Old Man, fearing for Faustus's soul, exits.

> **COMMENT:** The Old Man parallels the Good Angel of earlier scenes. He is a voice of good counsel or reason persuading man to avoid evil and the possibility of spiritual damnation. The association with the Morality Play is fairly obvious because of the analogy between the Old Man and the abstract personifications of moral good in that type drama. When Mephistophilis offers Faustus the dagger, he is urging him to the sin of despair, and he is acting contrary to the counsel of the Old Man. Here we see repeated again the basic struggle between God and the not-God, which before had been externalized in the Good versus Bad Angel debates.
>
> Notice, too, how Faustus' soliloquy poses the alternatives of Christ's mercy and despair. Faustus, aware of the horror of his sins, is led to recognize that mercy is still a possibility, though there is justice in the claim of hell because of his sin and the terms of his bargain. The contest is now between repentance and obdurateness, and Faustus so indicates:

> Accursed Faustus, where is mercy now?
> I do repent; and yet I do despair
> Hell strives with grace for conquest in my breast:
> What shall I do to shun the snares of death?

Mephistophilis threatens to tear Faustus to pieces for disobedience to Lucifer, and Faustus begs forgiveness by swearing to confirm his vow to Lucifer again with his blood. Faustus then asks Mephistophilis to torment the Old Man, whom he describes as "that base and aged man." Mephistophilis, knowing that he cannot afflict the Old Man's soul, says that he will try to hurt his body. At this point, Faustus asks Mephistophilis for a favor that is a high point in the play:

> One thing, good servant, let me crave of thee,
> To glut the longing of my heart's desire,—
> That I may have unto my paramour
> That heavenly Helen which I saw of late,
> Whose sweet embraces may extinguish clear
> Those thoughts that do dissuade me from my vow,
> And keep my oath I made to Lucifer.

Mephistophilis assures Faustus that this and all else he desires shall be performed in the "twinkling of an eye."

**COMMENT:**      Faustus by repeating the contract (signing his name on paper with his blood) reiterates his resolve to pursue "cursed necromancy" and to remain true to the bargain which surrenders his soul to Lucifer for eternity. Firmly in Lucifer's party, Faustus asks for a culminating favor: to have Helen of Troy for his paramour. According to legend, Helen was the great beauty over whom the Trojan War was fought. Note the effective diction in Faustus's speech ("crave," "glut," "extinguish") which indicates Faustus's sexual passion for a spirit. He desires that "her sweet embraces" may extinguish any thoughts of repentance, Christ's mercy, and salvation.

Helen enters and passes across the stage between two Cupids, and Faustus, captivated by the sight, delivers the most famous speech in the play:

> Was this the face that launch'd a thousand ships,
> And burnt the topless towers of Ilium?
> Sweet Helen, make me immortal with a kiss.—
>                  [She kisses him.]
> Her lips suck forth my soul: see where it flies!
> Come, Helen, come, give me my soul again.
> Here will I dwell, for heaven is in these lips,
> And all is dross that is not Helena.
> I will be Paris, and for love of thee,
> Instead of Troy, shall Wittenberg be sack'd;
> And I will combat with weak Menelaus,
> And wear thy colours on my plumed crest:

Yea, I will wound Achilles in the heel,
And then return to Helen for a kiss.
O, thou art fairer than the evening's air
Clad in the beauty of a thousand stars;
Brighter art thou than flaming Jupiter
When he appear'd to hapless Semele;
More lovely than the monarch of the sky
In wanton Arethusa's azured arms;
And none but thou shalt be my paramour!

**COMMENT:** Earlier, Alexander and Darius were impersonated by spirits, and in this scene Helen of Troy is impersonated by a spirit. Faustus begins by addressing a question to her; he asks if she is Helen, the cause of the Trojan War, about which Homer wrote his epic poem the *Iliad*. Helen's lips "suck forth" his soul to destruction. Demonic encounter was equated with bestiality by Renaissance commentators, and in this physical act with Helen we see a counterpart to the spiritual sin of selling one's soul. Faustus, inverting values, makes Helen his heaven ("heaven is in these lips"), and considers all "dross" (worthless metal) that is not Helen. Faustus continues in lyrical, evocative tones to recreate the world of Homer's *Iliad*, as he proceeds to vow "none but thou shalt be my paramour." Helen's beauty is compared to the divine splendor of Jupiter, whose flaming lightning consumed the hapless Semele when he appeared as a shepherd to her. The comparison is apt because the flaming passion of the demonic act with Helen will consume Faustus, who, like Semele, had also asked for this vision of beauty which, ironically, is destructive.

The poetry of these lines reveals magnificently Marlowe's mastery of blank verse (unrhymed iambic pentameter), and indeed these lines rival Shakespeare at his very best. It may be noted here that one of Marlowe's great contributions to the Elizabethan theater was his perfection of blank verse ("his mighty line"), which was to become the standard verse form for Shakespeare and his contemporaries.

Marlowe, in Faustus's lyrical apostrophe to Helen, reveals within the poetic context the aesthetic charm of a beauty destructive of all moral restraints. Faustus here utters the hyperboles of conventional love poetry to a friend who literally "sucks forth" his soul. The contrast between his lyrical vision and the gruesome fact of the demoniac mirrors the basic conflict of the play, which Marlowe has presented to us by his repetitive structure.

The Old Man, who has been standing to one side while Faustus speaks to Helen, says the following when Faustus, Helen, and the Cupids exit:

Accursed Faustus, miserable man
That from thy soul exclud'st the grace of Heaven,
And fliest the throne of his tribunal-seat!

The Devils enter to try the Old Man, but he defeats them because his faith conquers them. He cries out: "Hence, hell! for hence I fly unto my God."

COMMENT:    The Old Man, who has been associated with the allegorical personifications of the morality play, overcomes Lucifer and his devils here, and his victory is in contrast to Faustus's succumbing to diabolic powers. When he calls Faustus "accursed," he properly notes the fact that Faustus has rejected God and the possibility of repentance. Also, the Old Man's victory provides one more instance of the repetitive good versus evil combat.

SUMMARY:    In Act V, Scene One we see the following important events:

1. Faustus magically presents the spirit of Helen of Troy to the scholars who are enamored of her beauty.

2. The Old Man, a type of Good-Counsel figure, enters to advise Faustus to repent and call upon the mercy of Christ. The Morality play influence can be detected here because the Old Man parallels the role of the Good Angel in his play and

the role of many of the personified abstractions in morality-type drama. Faustus, however, is obdurate in his sin and is counselled to despair by Mephistophilis.

3. Faustus, fearing lest the devils tear him to pieces, signs the bargain again with his blood. Faustus parodies the shedding of Christ's blood through his blasphemous dedication to the not-God.

4. In this scene occurs the episode wherein Faustus copulates with the spirit of Helen of Troy, an act which seals Faustus's damnation. Faustus's apostrophe to Helen—"Was this the face that launch'd a thousand ships . . ."—recalls the Trojan Wars recounted by Homer in the *Iliad,* and this speech with its references to Paris, Achilles, Menelaus, and Troy brings to mind the tragic destruction caused long ago by Helen's beauty. Faustus's destruction, too, is caused by sensual lust for Helen, and Faustus, like Paris, shall die because Helen's lips literally "suck forth" his soul.

5. The Old Man overcomes the devils, and this marks a victory for the good in its war against sin. He departs from Faustus because Faustus is no longer capable of repentance; it is impossible for Faustus to achieve the spiritual victory which the Old Man counselled and won.

## ACT V: SCENE TWO

The scene opens in Faustus's study where Beelzebub and Mephistophilis watch unseen from above. Lucifer speaks first of how the devils ascend from hell to view those who, through sin, have sealed themselves "black sons of hell." Lucifer also says that Faustus's time has come and that lasting damnation awaits him. Mephistophilis tells them that Faustus is plagued by his conscience, that his brain begets "idle fantasies" in a desperate attempt to overreach the devil. All is in vain, Mephistophilis says, because Faustus's worldly pleasures must now be sauced with the pain of eternal damnation in hell. Faustus and his

servant Wagner enter, and Wagner tells Faustus that he is greatly pleased by his master's will. The Scholars then enter. They
note what they believe is melancholy in Faustus, but Faustus
says that it is: "a surfeit of deadly sin, that hath damn'd both
body and soul." The Second Scholar tells Faustus to call upon
God, and Faustus replies:

> On God, whom Faustus hath abjur'd! on God,
> whom Faustus hath blasphem'd! Oh, my God, I
> would weep! but the devil draws in my tears.
> Gush forth blood, instead of tears! yea, life
> and soul—Oh, he stays my tongue! I would lift
> up my hands; but see, they hold 'em, they hold 'em!

The Second Scholar again urges Faustus to call on God, but
Faustus, recalling his blasphemy against God, says the devils
draw back his tears of repentance, stay his tongue, and prevent
him from raising his hands to God. The Scholars ask who does
this to Faustus, and he replies: "Why, Lucifer and Mephistophilis. O, gentlemen, I gave them my soul for my cunning!"
The Scholars cry out in amazement. Faustus narrates the terms
of the contract, his fear of telling the Scholars because the devils
threatened to tear him to pieces, and finally he tells the
Scholars that "the date is expired." The Scholars exit to an ad-
joining room where they will pray for Faustus.

> **COMMENT:**      This scene is the prelude to the seizure of
> Faustus by the devils according to the contract. The recol-
> lection of his past career, his blasphemy against God, and
> his cunning serve to present Faustus's struggle in the in-
> tense heat of its conclusion. The hovering between re-
> pentance and the bargain is repeated again, but now Faustus
> says it is too late. When the scholars leave him, we may
> also note that learning and its powers have left Faustus to
> meet his destiny alone.

Mephistophilis speaks from above:

> Ay, Faustus, now thou hast no hope of heaven;
> Therefore despair, think only upon hell,
> For that must be thy mansion, there to dwell.

Faustus blames the "betwitching fiend" for tempting him, and Mephistophilis boastfully accepts his role and repeats to Faustus the counsel of despair. The Good and Bad Angel enter at different doors, and the Good Angel recalls that Faustus turned a deaf ear to its advice and instead loved the world. The Bad Angel tells Faustus that all his worldly pleasures and riches will now only serve to vex and to make him want in hell. A throne descends to the stage, and the Good Angel speaks:

O thou has lost celestial happiness,
Pleasures unspeakable, bliss without end.
Hadst thou affected sweet divinity,
Hell, or the devil, had had no power on thee.
Hadst thou kept on that way, Faustus, behold,
In what resplendent glory thou hadst sit
In yonder throne, like those bright shining saints,
And triumph'd over hell: that hast thou lost:
And now, poor soul, must thy good angel leave thee,
                    [The throne ascends.]
The jaws of hell are open to receive thee.

At the end of the Good Angel's speech, hell is discovered on the stage (apparently a curtain was drawn to reveal a painted dropcloth).

**COMMENT:**     Mephistophilis counsels Faustus to the ultimate sin for the Christian—despair, which denies the efficacy of Christ's mercy gained by the Redemption. The inability of Faustus to repent is despair, for it involves the hardening of the will against God through the habit of pride.

Faustus is so totally committed to the not-God that repentance is an impossibility, and here we recall his copulation with the spirit of Helen as the culminating sin of pride because it involved a "communion" with a demon. The appearance of the throne symbolizes Faustus' loss; the throne moves upward to leave Faustus alone in his "mansion" —the eternal fires of hell. Indeed, through sin, Faustus has built up his mansion in hell.

The throne probably descended by means of rope and pulleys in the Elizabethan theater, and the audience was certainly accustomed to associating the upper regions of the stage with Heaven. Hell was probably presented physically by use of a painted dropcloth, as mentioned previously, or by a trap which let forth fire and smoke when it was discovered. This physical contrast of heaven and hell obviously indicates the spiritual contrast of good and evil which is the basic theme of the play.

The Bad Angel then addresses Faustus and reveals to him the horrors of hell:

> Now, Faustus, let thine eyes with horror stare
> Into that vast perpetual torture-house.
> There are the Furies tossing damned souls
> On burning forks; their bodies boil in lead:
> There are live quarters broiling on the coals,
> That ne'er can die: This ever-burning chair
> Is for o'er-tortured souls to rest them in
> These that are fed with sops of flaming fire,
> Were gluttons and lov'd only delicates,
> And laugh'd to see the poor starve at their gates:
> But yet all these are nothing; thou shalt see
> Ten thousand tortures that more horrid be.

Faustus says that he has seen enough, and the Bad Angel tells him that soon he will taste the pain of all this because his time draws near. Hell disappears; the clock strikes eleven and the scene closes.

**COMMENT:**     The Bad Angel's speech on hell contrasts with that of the Good Angel. The presentation of the horrors of hell in the traditional terms of fire vividly reveals the eternity of suffering for which Faustus has bargained.

Faustus delivers his last great speech which traverses the last hour of his life and which sums up the themes of his spiritual conflict. He wishes that the revolving spheres might stand still, that time would cease, and that midnight, the fated hour, might never come. Faustus prays that there might yet be time for him to repent and to save his soul. His last great soliloquy reveals the torment of his final moments of life, and these lines also show Marlowe's superb use of blank verse:

> *O lente, lente currite, noctis equi!*
> The stars move still, time runs, the clock will strike,
> The devil will come, and Faustus must be damn'd.
> O, I'll leap up to my God! Who pulls me down?
> See, see, where Christ's blood streams in the firmament!
> One drop would save my soul, half a drop: ah, my Christ!
> Ah, rend not my heart for naming of my Christ!
> Yet will I call on him: O, spare me, Lucifer!—
> Where is it now? 'tis gone: and see, where God
> Stretcheth out his arm, and bends his ireful brows!
> Mountains and hills, come, come, and fall on me,
> And hide me from the heavy wrath of God!

Faustus wishes that he were changed into a mist so that his soul might ascend to heaven. The clock strikes the half hour, and Faustus asks that Christ might end his pain. Faced by the prospect of an eternity in hell, Faustus wishes that he had been a creature wanting soul. He refers to Pythagoras's theory of metempsychosis, the transmigration of souls, in the hope that he might be changed into some brutish beast. Faustus then curses the parents that bore him, and the clock strikes twelve. Faustus's final wish is that he might be dissolved into the elements of air and water to prevent Lucifer from bringing him to hell. Thunder strikes, and the devils enter to seize Faustus, whose words are those of a soul in anguish:

> My God, my God, look not so fierce on me!
> Adders and serpents, let me breathe a while!
> Ugly hell, gape not! come not, Lucifer!
> I'll burn my books!—Ah, Mephistophilis!

**COMMENT:** The initial lines of Faustus's last soliloquy express his wish that time might stand still so that he could repent and save his soul. *"O lente, lente currite, noctis equi!"* is quoted from Ovid, *Amores. I, xiii, Line* 40. Marlowe translated this in his *Ovid's Elegies*: "Then would'st thou cry, "Stay night, and run not thus!" The lover in Ovid wishes to prolong the night so that he may remain with his mistress (see John Donne's poems "The Sunne Rising" and

"Breake of Day"). The irony here has been noted often; Faustus, like the lover, finds that time is his enemy and pleasure must end. But the lover may return to the arms of his mistress, and Faustus is denied this possibility. His bargain has been made out of love for pleasure and power, but now Faustus must face the inescapable fact that he must pay the price for rejecting God.

This monologue is one of the finest passages of poetry in the entire play, for here Marlowe uses a colloquial rhythm within the blank verse line to suggest the torment within Faustus's soul. The tone here is quite different from the lyrical apostrophe to Helen, and this is as it should be because Marlowe is attempting here to show the agony of Faustus in his final hour. During the final hour of his life, Faustus again thinks of repentance and he sees Christ's blood as it "streams in the firmament." But his former fear, that the devils will punish him for recanting, again overcomes Faustus and he cries: "Ah, rend not my heart for naming of my Christ!" Aware of his horrible sins, Faustus wishes that mountains would hide him from the face of God, and he also wishes that he were turned into a soulless beast. Faustus wishes that he were anything but a man, so that he might escape the punishment that awaits him. As the God of justice looks down upon him, the devils enter to bring Faustus to hell. He asks "ugly" hell to gape not, and the word ugly is an important one, for thus Faustus described Mephistophilis when he first summoned him from hell. Faustus's life of sin and of delusive pleasure has been replaced by the final reality. His soul in all its ugliness is taken to hell where Faustus, like Mephistophilis, will feel the torment of ten thousand hells in being deprived of everlasting bliss. Faustus's plea, "My God, my God look not so fierce on me!" is the cry of a damned soul and it calls to mind the words of *Psalm XXII*: "My God, my God, why hast thou forsaken me? why art thou so far from helping me, and from the words of my roaring?"

**SUMMARY:**　　　Act V, Scene 2 presents the final hours of Faustus's life and reveals his torment as his allotted time draws to a close. He tosses between thoughts of repentance and the inescapable fact of his destined end in hell fire. Mephistophilis counsels Faustus to despair, and Faustus rejects the celestial throne of the Good Angel for the horrors of hell described by the Bad Angel. Faustus, during the last hours of his life, desperately wishes that time would stand still, that he might dissolve into the elements of air and water; however, all is in vain because the devils come to seize him at the appointed hour. Earlier, in Act I, Scene 1, Faustus had spoken of his "desperate enterprise," and at the end of the play we see him truly desperate. The word desperate is connected with despair, the loss of hope; theologically, despair means the ultimate sin for the Christian, the loss of hope in the possibility of salvation. Faustus has chosen to reject God, and now despair is his lot. Ironically what Faustus has willed to be has happened, for he has sold his soul into an eternity of suffering.

## ACT V: SCENE THREE

The Scholars enter and after noting the fearful shrieks that they have heard this night, they find Faustus's limbs all torn apart by the hand of death. The Third Scholar says that between the hours of twelve and one he heard Faustus shrieking and that the devils whom Faustus served have done this to the great Doctor. The Second Scholar then promises Faustus a proper burial because Faustus once was a greatly admired scholar in German schools.

## EPILOGUE

An Epilogue, or short speech by way of conclusion, is spoken by the Chorus:

> Cut is the branch that might have grown full straight,
> And burned is Apollo's laurel-bough,
> That sometime grew within this learned man.
> Faustus is gone: regard his hellish fall,
> Whose fiendful fortune may exhort the wise,
> Only to wonder at unlawful things,
> Whose deepness doth entice such forward wits
> To practise more than heavenly power permits.
> *Terminat hora diem; terminat Author opus.*

**COMMENT:**     The source of the first line of the Epilogue is probably Thomas Churchyard's popular tragedy "Shore's Wife" in *The Mirror for Magistrates,* where the ghost of Mistress Shore places the blame upon her friends who "brake the boughs and shaked the tree by sleight,/ And bent the wand that might have grown full straight."

The reference to Apollo is to the god of wisdom, and Faustus, the Epilogue points out, has been destroyed because he put his great learning to improper use. Faustus's learning did not grow straight, but instead he pursued "cursed necromancy" and rejected his "chiefest bliss." The exhortation of the Epilogue to the audience is that Faustus's "hellish fall" should teach men not to be enticed forward to investigate and know what heaven forbids. The Latin quote is translated: "The hour ends the day; the author ends his work."

# CHARACTER ANALYSES

**DOCTOR FAUSTUS:** Doctor Faustus is the central figure in the play and dominates the entire action. He is a man who has mastered human learning, but who, like Icarus, attempts to go beyond human limitations in a quest for knowledge. Having risen from humble origins to a position of eminence at the University of Wittenberg, Faustus is yet not content. He finds law, theology, medicine, and philosophy too "illiberal". Faustus desires the freedom (the Latin word, *liberus*) to pursue the study of necromancy, or black magic. Ironically, this freedom involves really a kind of bondage because Faustus must shed his blood to seal a contract for his soul with Lucifer in order to gain the powers of magic. Rejecting "submission" to God, Faustus chooses to be like a god himself, and thus, he enters his fatal contract. Throughout the play we see Faustus repeatedly confronted by the choice of God or the not-God, and repeatedly Faustus confirms his contract by electing the not-God. Marlowe, by the cumulative effect of the repeated episodes wherein we see Faustus opting for "cursed necromancy," creates a tragic figure of considerable strength. Faustus's magical career presents a vivid illustration of the impotence of his magical powers because, as we see in the comic portions of the play, Faustus becomes no more than a practical-joker. The tremendous gap between Faustus's imaginative dreams of the glories that will result from magic and the vacuous reality that results provides by way of irony a telling comment on the nature of his bargain. Faustus is a man possessed with an aspiring mind; he is the individualist at odds with orthodox religion. When Faustus commits a demoniac act with a spirit representing Helen of Troy, we are witness to his final blasphemy against God, and by this act Faustus seals his damnation. His tragedy, then, is that of a man who would be more than human, who would be like a god. Faustus's final speech reveals his awareness of the consequences of his choice, as he desperately tries to avert the catastrophe that awaits him. His is a spiritual tragedy fought within the soul of man, and in Faustus we see the universal conflict between forces of good and evil, reason and passion, salvation and damnation. Impelled by aspiration for knowledge, Faustus tragically comes to know human limitation, suffering, and the horror of the greatest isolation—to be without God. Ironically, in trying to become more than human, Faustus at the end of his life rejects his humanity and wishes that he had been a beast, a creature wanting discourse of reason. He wishes that he were dissolved into elemental nothingness so that he might escape the torment of hell. There is at the end of *Doctor Faustus* a sense of tragic waste in that we see greatness destroyed; however, we are also aware that Faustus gained what he chose.

**MEPHISTOPHILIS:**    A devil sent by Lucifer, the chief devil, to assist Faustus during the twenty-four years of his bargain. Mephistophilis serves Faustus by showing him the Seven Deadly Sins, Helen of Troy, and by enabling Faustus to learn the secrets of the universe. Through Mephistophilis Faustus practices the magic which is ultimately to damn him. Also Mephistophilis serves to prevent Faustus from going back on his bargain. Thus, whenever Faustus thinks of repenting, Mephistophilis quickly threatens him with physical destruction. The temporal alliance of Faustus and Mephistophilis foreshadows the eternity that they will spend together in hell.

**THE GOOD AND BAD ANGELS:**    These are personified abstractions from the Morality play tradition. They reappear in *Doctor Faustus* as external representations of the inner forces contending for Faustus's soul. These characters are engaged in a debate, as it were, and the prize is Faustus's soul.

**THE OLD MAN:**    He appears at the end of the play to utter a final appeal to Faustus to repent and call upon the mercy of Christ. His message is the same as that of the Good Angel, and in many ways the Old Man resembles a morality abstraction such as Good Counsel. When Faustus rejects the advice of the Old Man, the devils make an attempt against the Old Man. However, in contrast to Faustus, the Old Man overcomes his tempters and thereby shows the possibility of spiritual victory and the power of grace.

**WAGNER:** He is Faustus's servant, to whom the learned Doctor wills all his wealth in Act V. Wagner, in Act I, parodies his master by conjuring two devils so that he may persuade a Clown to serve him. Wagner's action on a comic plane indicates the accessibility of magic even to the unlearned and provides a satiric comment on the main action, particularly when we have in mind Faustus's lyric and imaginative exaltation of the powers of magic.

**ROBIN AND DICK:** These two minor characters are part of the comic sub-plot. When Robin finds a book on magic, he gives up his job as a stableman. Robin and Dick steal a goblet and conjure Mephistophilis to bring it back to the vintner's boy. For this action Robin and Dick are punished by Mephistophilis and Faustus. Again, this action acts as a satiric and comic contrast to the main plot.

**BENVOLIO:** He is the knight who doubts the magical powers of Faustus, and as a punishment Faustus places cuckold's horns on his head. When Benvolio, with Frederick and Martino, seeks to revenge himself against Faustus, he is thwarted by Faustus and all three are punished. Benvolio is involved in that portion of the play which reveals the magical powers of Faustus, and it is seen that Faustus is really a practical-joker.

**THE HORSE-COURSER:** He is a horse-dealer, whose profession had a notorious reputation for shady deals. In a comic action Faustus outwits him by selling him a horse which turns into hay upon being ridden into water. He is later struck dumb by Faustus when he attempts to tell his tale of woe.

**VALDES AND CORNELIUS:**    These are two scholars who are learned in the ways of necromancy. They are friends of Faustus and are instrumental in persuading him to follow "cursed necromancy."

**BRUNO:**    He is the anti-Pope who is released from captivity in Rome by Faustus and Mephistophilis. The Emperor of Germany receives Bruno back again, and praises Faustus for his actions.

**MINOR CHARACTERS:**    *Doctor Faustus* is crowded with minor personages who serve simply as comic foils or as personified representations of good or evil. Among the former are the VINTNER'S BOY, who engages in a comic scene with Robin and Dick when he tries to regain his master's goblet. The FRIARS and CARDINALS attending the Pope are also the objects of Faustus's horseplay while in Rome. The POPE, who has captured Bruno, is also the object of Faustus's pranks. Faustus slaps the Pope, steals his dish, and also deceives him over Bruno and the sentence of the Consistory. Among the personified abstractions are the SEVEN DEADLY SINS, who appear to Faustus and delight his soul. HELEN OF TROY, described by the SCHOLARS as the most beautiful woman who ever lived, appears as a spirit representing the real Helen; Faustus commits a demoniac act with this spirit. THE CHORUS acts as prologue providing narrative material, and at the end delivers the Epilogue containing a moral about how necessary it is not to be overly curious in quest of knowledge.

# CRITICAL COMMENTARY

Marlowe's *Doctor Faustus* has been accepted by most critics to be his finest tragedy, and critical writing about the play has focused upon its important contribution to the development and history of English tragedy. Popular in its own time, *Doctor Faustus* continues to fascinate readers and audiences today because its subject is the clash between intellectual curiosity and orthodox restraints. Faustus in his person embodies human aspirations which when pushed beyond certain limits were deemed sinful. Marlowe, like Faustus, was, as has been seen from his biography, suspected during his life of religious skepticism, atheism, and free-thinking. Contemporary references make Marlowe out to be a blasphemer who flouted religious orthodoxy. Though much of Marlowe's biography remains shrouded in the dense fog of political intrigue, it seems that Marlowe was certainly an outspoken intellectual of his day. Critics, seizing upon this and other details of Marlowe's life, have frequently looked to Marlowe's plays as illustrations of Marlowe's unorthodox opinions and beliefs. Thus, tragic heroes like Tamburlaine and Faustus are viewed as "spokesmen" for Marlowe's personal views. This critical position may be labelled the subjective approach, for it views the plays as personal vehicles for the playwright's attitudes. Opposed to this view is the objective approach which makes a distinction between what Marlowe personally thought and what he has his characters think.

The subjective view is represented by Paul H. Kocher's *Christopher Marlowe: A Study of His Thought, Learning and Character* (1946). Kocher maintains that Marlowe was a highly subjective dramatist who emphasized the ideas of power and force in his plays. Tamburlaine, for instance, is viewed by Kocher as a Scourge of God punishing by force and achieving regal power by force, which is the law of nature and of man. There is a valuable section in Kocher's book which treats the importance of religion to Marlowe's imagination. Kocher believes that Marlowe's struggle with Christianity was the fountain of his literary genius. Chapters on Witchcraft, Astronomy and Meteorology, and Politics and Ethics provide invaluable information for an understanding of Marlowe's learning and his age. Kocher's general approach is reflected in the following quote: "The story of the plays, as we have seen, is the story of the fate of the doctrine of *Sic volo, sic jubeo,* stately and proud in the morning, and in the evening fallen so low beneath a rising conception of personal and social justice." Marlowe's tragic heroes then are viewed as kinds of supermen defiantly asserting "Thus I wish, thus I command," and the dramatic progression is from the proud Tamburlaine, the aspiring Faustus, to the more socially conscious and less defiant Edward II. The emphasis in Kocher's study is upon the presence of Machiavellian *virtú,* the ability to achieve and hold power, in Marlowe's plays.

Harry Levin in *The Overreacher: A Study of Christopher Marlowe* (1952) aptly indicates the important contribution that Marlowe made to Elizabethan drama through his mastering of the blank verse line. The rhythmic line of Marlowe, with its characteristic middle pause, its sonority, its use of polysyllabic words, and resonant use of proper names, as in Faustus's apostrophe to Helen, greatly influenced later dramatists. The following quote from *Tamburlaine Part I* illustrates several of these features: "That perfect bliss and sole felicity,/ The sweet fruition of an earthly crown." Marlowe's use of hyperbole, a figure of thought and style, is the characteristic mode of Marlovian tragedy, and, according to Levin, accounts for Marlowe's interest in the exceptional man, the man who is an "overreacher." It is the hero's assertion of man's will rather than the acceptance of God's will that makes for tragedy in Marlowe's plays. Levin finds in Marlowe's life and work an insight into the life of an individualist who lives without control. Faustus, who aspired like Icarus, is thus an "overreacher" asserting individual freedom, and Faustus becomes the mythic embodiment of the shift from the Medieval-Renaissance metaphysical plane to the literal plane of naturalism. Levin's study, then, is an important contribution to the subjective critical approach to Marlowe.

Roy W. Battenhouse in *Marlowe's Tamburlaine: A Study in Renaissance Moral Philosophy* (1941) takes exception to the subjective approach because he believes such markedly romantic criticism abolishes the distinction between drama and autobiography. Battenhouse cites the works of U. M. Ellis-Fermor, *Christopher Marlowe* (1927), and F. S. Boas, *Christopher Marlowe* (1940), as pertinent examples of the tendency to take what is said in the plays for Marlowe's personal opinions and beliefs. Some of the pitfalls of romantic criticism are avoided by John Bakeless in *Christopher Marlowe* (1937). Bakeless indicates that Machiavellianism is the historic source of the titan spirit in Tamburlaine and Marlowe's other tragic heroes. However, as Battenhouse points out, Bakeless, though not admiring Tamburlaine's ethical philosophy, falls into the romantic pitfall of identifying Tamburlaine with Marlowe. A commonsense approach is advocated by Battenhouse, who sees Marlowe's *Tamburlaine* as a moral spectacle which represents the protest of traditional, orthodox ethics against Renaissance individualism. From a study of the background of the morality play, Elizabethan history, moral philosophy, literary theory, and religious apologetics, Battenhouse concludes that ambition is Tamburlaine's tragic flaw and that Marlowe, together with his audience, viewed ambition as sinful, in accord with orthodox religious and ethical writings. While Battenhouse's book is specifically concerned with *Tamburlaine,* it marks an important shift of emphasis from the romantic approach to a more objective evaluation of Marlowe's work.

A good deal of recent critical work in Renaissance drama has emphasized the native elements in the growth of English popular drama. David M. Bevington's *From Mankind to Marlowe: Growth of Structure in the Popular Drama of Tudor England* (1962) is an extremely important study along these lines. Bevington emphasizes the influence of the popular morality play and hybrid forms upon the development of drama in England. Plays such as *Cambises* contain the essential elements which produce a kind of drama wherein such figures as Faustus, Tamburlaine, and Richard III (Shakespeare) dominate the scene, and Marlowe derived his episodic structure from the moral and hybrid chronicle. Bevington analyzes the structure of Marlowe's plays from this point of view, and he indicates the relevance of the comic sub-plot, which parodies Faustus's sins, to the theme of the play. *Doctor Faustus* is seen as the presentation of a spiritual life, and all events concentrate on the question of salvation or damnation. Several major phases are present in the structure or plan of the play: plotting and temptation, downfall and spiritual struggle, degeneracy, and damnation. Bevington's study, then, is a singularly significant contribution to our understanding of the structure of Marlowe's plays and their obvious debt to the older morality drama. The plot of *Doctor Faustus* emphasizes the tragic and destructive side of the morality or Psycho-machia (conflict between good and evil) drama and shows us the rewards of sin—death.

*Suffering and Evil in the Plays of Christopher Marlowe* (1962) by Douglas Cole approaches Marlowe's plays from a thorough grounding in the background of medieval mystery cycles, the morality play, *De Casibus* tragedy, and Senecan tragedy. Cole stresses Marlowe's theological sophistication, which is well-taken because the Cambridge of Marlowe's time was a center for theological learning and controversy. This theological learning, Cole writes, undoubtedly contributed to Marlowe's artistic vision of tragedy, and it certainly helped shape his attitude towards suffering and evil, the prime concerns of tragic drama. Marlowe's plays, in Cole's view, must also be experienced in and for themselves without looking to them to find out about Marlowe's personal life and without reducing them simply to interesting pieces preparing the way for Shakespeare. Marlowe's focus in *Doctor Faustus* is upon one man who through his own choice brings suffering and damnation down upon his head. As Cole points out, the irony in *Doctor Faustus* is based on theological concepts of sin and damnation, and this penetrating irony is dramatically expressed in two controlling patterns of action: ". . . the repetitive pattern of moral choice leading to the alternative of spiritual destruction, and the pattern of contrast between Faustus's grand imaginative designs and the actual, vacuous accomplishments of his magical career." (P. 191) Faustus, in this tragedy, suffers what in theological terms is called *poena damni;* the punishment of loss. Ironically what he has willed he ultimately obtains, and Faustus is damned to remain eternally in that state which he freely chose. From an awareness of Marlowe's theological learning, Cole concludes that no matter what Marlowe's personal views of Christianity were, it is clear that in *Doctor Faustus* he ". . . has fashioned a play that is thoroughly Christian in conception and import."

Critical essays on Marlowe multiply yearly in the scholarly journals and testify to his continued importance. Only a few of these essays may be mentioned here, however. Lily B. Campbell looks upon Marlowe's *Doctor Faustus* as the dramatization of a case of conscience such as fascinated Protestant theologians in the sixteenth century. Her essay, *"Doctor Faustus*: A Case of Conscience" (*PMLA, LXVII* [1952], 219-239) uses a case dramatized in *The Conflict of Conscience* (1581) by N. Woods to parallel that in *Doctor Faustus.*

Countering the romantic view, James Smith in "Marlowe's *Doctor Faustus"* (Scrutiny, VIII [1939-40], 36-55) states the opinion that the play is an allegory with an orthodox Christian attitude towards Faustus's career. W. W. Greg in "The Damnation of Faustus" (*MLR,* XLI[1946], 97-107) writes on Faustus's sin of demoniality with Helen and provides theological texts on the subject.

Helen Gardner in "Milton's 'Satan' and the Theme of Damnation" (*English Studies,* n.s., I[1948], 46-66) treats *Doctor Faustus, Macbeth,* and Thomas Middleton's *The Changeling.* All three plays are concerned with evildoers who are not capable of repentance, and in all three cases the initial sin is against nature. Faustus rejects God and deliberately wills to sell his soul to Lucifer. The three plays also have in common the irony of retributive justice, for in all three cases something forbidden, though seemingly desirable, is willed for, and the achievement of desire brings with it suffering and torment. J. C. Maxwell in "The Plays of Christopher Marlowe" (in *The Age of Shakespeare,* 1955) gives strong support to the fact that Marlowe's *Doctor Faustus* reflects traditional attitudes when he writes:

> The overt meaning of the play has given offence
> to some of those who are convinced that the
> accounts of Marlowe's anti-Christian views
> are to be taken very seriously, and also that
> Marlowe was determined to give expression to those
> views in his plays. I do not know what Marlowe's
> religious beliefs were when he wrote this play,
> but there is nothing in it which could not have
> been written by a convinced Christian: he does
> not twist the traditional story for anti-traditional
> ends. (P. 169)

Marlowe's *Doctor Faustus* is then the tragedy of a man who tries to go beyond the limits of human knowledge. Faustus's tragedy is one of the spirit because his suffering is not physical but the spiritual loss of eternal bliss. Tragedy, as a literary genre, is concerned with the facts of pain and suffering in life, and with human isolation and finitude. *Doctor Faustus,* too, is so centered, for Faustus chooses "cursed necromancy" at the expense of eternal bliss. The tragic irony of the play is that Faustus's own choice is the cause for the ultimate suffering visited upon him. The choice of worldly pleasure also involves spiritual loss, the deprivation of the eternal joys of heaven. If we speak in Aristotelian terms, then Faustus's *hamartia* or tragic flaw resides in his pride and ambition, in his attempt to be like a God. Faustus's sin is like that of Lucifer, for it involves rebellion and rejection of God. In rejecting God, Faustus is finally left to despair and hopelessness. The spiritual career of Faustus is the story of the greatly learned man who wanders into the forbidden ways of necromancy. Faustus's will elects the not-God, and as a result of this choice Faustus surrenders his soul to destruction.

The Faust story has become a myth which embodies the human desire for knowledge. Often the myth is looked upon as the embodiment of a satanic quest for forbidden knowledge, and critics have not been reluctant to see in Marlowe's *Doctor Faustus* the Renaissance humanist spirit striving against orthodox restraints. Marlowe's personal life combined with the subject matter and kinds of tragic heroes in his plays, it is believed, reveal the Renaissance struggle for freedom. Basil Willey, for instance, in his *The Seventeenth Century Background* (1934) writes of the rejection of scholasticism and the emergence of Baconian science and the inductive method in the seventeenth century. Willey describes traditional attitudes toward science as Mephistophilian, and the Faustus legend, he notes, revealed the traditional dread of the satanic powers of science.

E. M. Butler in *The Fortunes of Faust* (1952) treats the origin and history of the Faust legend. Marlowe's knowledge of black magic, perhaps derived from Reginald Scot's *Discoverie of Witchcraft* (1584), is discussed in reference to the conjuring scenes. Extremely valuable in this study is the treatment of later versions of the story. *Faust* by Johan Wolfgang Goethe (1749-1832) is a long, philosophical, dramatic poem wherein Faust goes through a series of temptations proposed by Mephistopheles, but Faust at the end of his life is victorious. At the end angels carry Faust to heaven, and Mephistopheles is defeated. Goethe's poem is an extremely important instance of the romantic attitude in literature. Charles Gounod's opera *Faust* was performed in 1859 and was based on Goethe's version of the legend. In the opera, the aged Faust signs a contract with Mephistopheles so that he may gain youth. At the end of the opera Marguerite, Faust's beloved, abhors the fiend and rejects Faust, and she is carried off to heaven by an angelic host. Faust is taken to hell by Mephistopheles. Thomas Mann (1875-1955), the German novelist and author of *The Magic Mountain,* also used the Faust myth in his novel *Doctor Faustus* (1949). The central figure in Mann's novel is Adrian Leverkühn, a sickly musical genius.

# BRIEF SUMMARY OF *TAMBURLAINE*

# *THE GREAT:* PART I

## DRAMATIC CHARACTERS

**MYCETES:**   King of Persia, a weak ruler.

**COSROE:**   Brother to Mycetes; he seizes rule of Persia and the Eastern Empire.

**ORTYGIUS:**
**MEANDER:**   All are Persian lords and captains and allies of Cosroe when he seizes power.
**MENAPHON:**

**THERIDAMAS:**   Persian Lord who deserts Cosroe for Tamburlaine. Tamburlaine crowns him King of Argier.

**TAMBURLAINE:**   The central figure of the play. A bloody tyrant who rises from a Scythian shepherd to become a powerful ruler. He is the Scourge of God.

**TECHELLES:**   Follower of Tamburlaine, later crowned King of Fez.

**USUMCASANE:**   Follower of Tamburlaine, later crowned King of Morocco.

**BAJAZETH:**   Emperor of the Turks who is defeated by Tamburlaine. He is treated inhumanly by Tamburlaine.

**KING OF ARABIA:**   Betrothed to Zenocrate; he dies in her arms after defeat by Tamburlaine.

**KING OF FEZ:** ⎫ Three great kings allied to Baja-
**KING OF ARGIER:** ⎬ zeth. They are also defeated by
**KING OF MOROCCO:** ⎭ Tamburlaine.

**SOLDAN OF EGYPT:** Zenocrate's father. At first he is an enemy of Tamburlaine's, but he is later reconciled.

**GOVERNOR OF DAMASCUS:** Ruler of the besieged city who sends four virgins to Tamburlaine to ask mercy.

**AGYDAS:** ⎫
**MAGNETES:** ⎬ Median lords in attendance on Zenocrate.

**CAPOLIN:** An Egyptian lord in the company of the Sultan.

**PHILEMUS:** A messenger.

**ZENOCRATE:** Daughter of the Sultan of Egypt. After her capture by Tamburlaine, she becomes his great love.

**ANIPPE:** Zenocrate's maid.

**ZABINA:** Bajazeth's wife; she suffers greatly with her husband as a result of Tamburlaine's cruelty.

**EBEA:** Zabina's maid.

**VIRGINS OF DAMASCUS:** They are sent to Tamburlaine by the Governor of Damascus to ask the tyrant for mercy; however, they are murdered.


## TAMBURLAINE THE GREAT: PART ONE


Mycetes, King of Persia, confers with his lords and captains and sends Theridamas with an army to suppress Tamburlaine, the upstart Scythian, who threatens Persia. Cosroe, brother of Mycetes, criticizes the folly of the King, and the King threatens revenge for his brother's contemptuous words. Ortygius and Oeneus present the crown to Cosroe who accepts because of his awareness of threatened dangers to Persia from without and from within. The ineffectual rule of Mycetes, the Persian warriors' demand for action, and the pleas of Menaphon, Oeneus, and Ortygius all persuade Cosroe to seize rule as Emperor of Asia and Persia. Tamburlaine, meanwhile, has captured Zenocrate, daughter of the Sultan of Egypt and the betrothed of the King of Arabia, and he has brought her to the Scythian camp. Tamburlaine woos Zenocrate and after telling her of his dreams of conquest and his intention to be lord of Asia, he promises her great riches; the final great gift is to be Tamburlaine himself. News is brought to Tamburlaine of the approaching Persian army which outnumbers Tamburlaine two to one. Theridamas enters and speaks when he sees Tamburlaine:

A Scythian shepherd so embellishe'd
With nature's pride and richest furniture!
His looks do menace Heaven and dare the gods.

Tamburlaine asks Theridamas to forsake his king and join with Tamburlaine, who will conquer the world. Tamburlaine speaks of himself as being favored by Jove, as one destined to shake off his obscurity and become lord of the world. Theridamas, greatly moved by Tamburlaine's persuasions, and impressed by his display of treasure, joins his forces with the Scythian's. Agydas and Magnetes, Median Lords captured with Zenocrate, yield their services to Tamburlaine, and Zenocrate admits she must accept her wretched state.

## ACT II

Cosroe is so impressed by the power of Tamburlaine that he decides to cooperate with him, and Tamburlaine assents to help Cosroe become Emperor of Asia. When Tamburlaine defeats Mycetes, Cosroe crowns Tamburlaine Regent of Persia and "general lieutenant of my armies." Meander, counsellor to

Mycetes, is taken into Cosroe's service. After Cosroe sets out with his forces to regain the Indian mines which his brother lost to the Christians, Tamburlaine begins to think of the glories of being a king. Tamburlaine tells Theridamas, Usum-casane and Techelles, his followers, of his plan to seize the crown from Cosroe. Cosroe, Ortygius, and Meander resolve to meet with force the presumption and ungrateful ambition of Tamburlaine. But Cosroe is defeated by the bloody Tam-burlaine, who in one of the most famous speeches in the works of Marlowe, talks of his aspiring ambition and his chief joy:

> The thirst of reign and sweetness of a crown
> That caused the eldest son of heavenly Ops,
> To thrust his doting father from his chair,
> And place himself in the empyreal Heaven,
> Moved me to manage arms against thy state.
> What better precedent than mighty Jove?
> Nature that framed us of four elements,
> Warring within our breasts for regiment,
> Doth teach us all to have aspiring minds:
> Our souls, whose faculties can comprehend
> The wondrous architecture of the world,
> And measure every wandering planet's course,
> Still climbing after knowledge infinite,
> And always moving as the restless spheres,
> Wills us to wear ourselves, and never rest,
> Until we reach the ripest fruit of all,
> The perfect bliss and sole felicity,
> The sweet fruition of an earthly crown.

Cosroe dies, the victim of Tamburlaine's thirst for reign. Usumcasane, Techelles, and Theridamas, who hope to gain kingdoms, all proclaim Tamburlaine King of Persia.

## ACT III

While Tamburlaine overhears, Zenocrate confesses to Agydas that she loves Tamburlaine. Agydas expresses displeasure that Zenocrate should love such a rude barbarian. Tamburlaine

enters and takes Zenocrate away by the hand, but before
he leaves he reveals displeasure at Agydas. Tamburlaine sends
a naked dagger to Agydas, and Agydas stabs himself to death.
Bajazeth, Emperor of the Turks, meanwhile realizes the threat
of Tamburlaine and offers a truce so that he may continue
the siege of Constantinople. However, Tamburlaine defies Bajazeth, the Bassoes, his followers, and the Kings of Fez, Morocco,
and Argier. Bajazeth places his crown on his wife Zabina's
head, and he tells her to wait until he returns victorious. Tamburlaine places his crown on Zenocrate's head and tells her to
wait with Zabina for his return. While the armies battle, Zenocrate and Zabina trade insults. Bajazeth is overcome by Tamburlaine, and Tamburlaine bids Zenocrate to take the Turkish
crown from Zabina and to crown him Emperor of Africa.
Tamburlaine refuses to accept ransom for his prisoners, Bajazeth and Zabina, and after dreaming of extending his rule
throughout the world, Tamburlaine orders a martial feast
to celebrate his victory.

## ACT IV

The Sultan of Egypt rouses the "men of Memphis" from their
torpor and joins with the King of Arabia to save his daughter
Zenocrate. The Sultan is told by a messeenger how Tamburlaine strikes terror into his enemies. It is Tamburlaine's custom to fly flags of white (mildness), red (blood), and black
(death and destruction); these are threats to cities and they
are flown on three successive days. Tamburlaine leaves the
city the choice of their manner of submission. While Tamburlaine waits for Damascus to submit, he commands that his
footstool be brought before him. Tamburlaine treats his prisoner Bajazeth inhumanly by keeping him in a cage and then
by using him for a footstool to ascend his royal throne. Zabina
suffers the indignity of having to feed the scraps left after
meals to the caged Bajazeth. After taunting Bajazeth and Zabina
at a banquet on a day when a red flag flies from his tent before the walls of Damascus, Tamburlaine is prevailed upon by
Zenocrate to grant her wish that the lives of her father and

friends be spared at Damascus. Tamburlaine softens to the extent that he agrees on the condition that they yield to him as their Emperor. Tamburlaine then crowns Theridamas, King of Argier; Techelles, King of Fez; and Usumcasane, King of Morocco.

## ACT V

On the third day of the siege of Damascus, Tamburlaine displays his black colors, and the Governor of the city, hoping to avert sure disaster, sends four virgins bearing laurel branches (symbolic of peace) to sue for pity from Tamburlaine. However, Tamburlaine has the virgins murdered and then hangs their bodies on the walls of the city. Tamburlaine then delivers a lyric apostrophe on his love for Zenocrate. Bajazeth, suffering from his present animal-like state and aware of Zabina's wretchedness, sends his wife to bring him a glass of water, and while she is gone, he dashes his brains out against his cage. When Zabina discovers her husband's body, she too dashes her brains out against the cage. Zenocrate comes upon the bodies of the Turkish Emperor and his Queen, and she laments this bloody spectacle and the slaughter of the Egyptians in Damascus. Zenocrate says that Bajazeth's face offers a lesson on the nature of earthly pomp and slippery crowns. She is also troubled by the conflict between love for her father and for Tamburlaine who are now preparing to meet in battle. The King of Arabia enters wounded and dies in Zenocrate's arms. The Sultan is led in a prisoner and is reunited with his daughter Zenocrate. The Sultan, however, is spared by Tamburlaine who then crowns Zenocrate Queen of Persia. Thus the play ends on this note of accord.

> **COMMENT:** Marlowe's sources for the Tamburlaine story were the Spaniard Pedro Mexia's *Silva de Varia Leccion* (1544) translated into English by Thomas Fortescue as *The Forest* (1571; 1576), *Magni Tamerlanis Scytharum Imperatoris Vita* ("The Life of Tamburlaine the Great, General of the Scythians") by Petrus Perondinus,

and numerous other chronicles. As the Prologue to Part II indicates, *Tamburlaine Part I* and *Part II* should be treated as individual works though they are related in subject and general treatment. In *Tamburlaine Part I* Marlowe has written a chronicle play which presents the story of the rise of the Scythian shepherd Tamburlaine from lowly origins to great power and majesty. Combining features of the morality play and the hybrid chronicle (for example, *Cambyses*), Marlowe presents an episodic panorama of the bloody career of a tyrant who thirsts for earthly glory. *Part I* traces Tamburlaine's rise by presenting his conquest of Persia, the Turkish Empire, and Damascus. The central theme of *Tamburlaine, Part I* is ambition: "The thirst of reign and sweetness of a crown. . . ." In Tamburlaine we have the portrait of a tyrant whose bloody deeds make him a kind of superman. He is an exponent of Machiavellian *virtù,* for he knows no other law than that of force. Nature has instructed Tamburlaine to have an aspiring mind and to seek "The perfect bliss and sole felicity,/ The sweet fruition of an earthly crown."

Acts I and II focus upon Persia. Here Tamburlaine defeats the weak and ineffectual Mycetes, King of Persia, and the embodiment of all that Tamburlaine's character despises. Tamburlaine's use of deceit to overcome Cosroe reveals the tyrant's *virtù*. Along with war, love is the main subject of *Tamburlaine, Part I,* and Zenocrate is another conquest for the aspiring Tamburlaine. Act III centers upon his conquest of the Turkish Empire and the capture of Bajazeth and Zabina. Acts IV and V concern the attack against Damascus and provide another episode in the military conquests of Tamburlaine. Throughout the play there are numerous instances to reveal Tamburlaine's cruelty, but this is nowhere more evident than in the barbaric treatment of Bajazeth and Zabina. Their deaths in Act V offer visual testimony to Tamburlaine's ruthlessness and cruelty.

Marlowe in *Tamburlaine, Part I* presents a series of episodes which are thematically united and which cumulatively indicate the ambitions and cruel nature of the central figure—Tamburlaine. The stately rhetoric, the imagery which suggests grandeur, the symbolic concentration upon "crowns," "jewels," "treasure," and recurrent use of classical mythology are all part of Marlowe's technique to present a superhuman character.

Interpretations of the play range from readings which see *Tamburlaine, Part I* as the embodiment of Marlowe's aspiring individualism to rigid moral views of Tamburlaine as the "Scourge of God" punishing God's enemies. Certainly the note of accord and the success of Tamburlaine in Act V vary the traditional *de casibus* pattern from defeat to victory, if we consider the first play apart from its sequel. Yet the ending may better be viewed as paradoxical, as not offering a resolution of problems, because we are left on the one hand with the double vision of the loftiness of Tamburlaine's rhetoric and of his titanic successes, and on the other hand we see the inhuman suffering and horror that has accompanied "The sweet fruition of an earthly crown."

# BRIEF SUMMARY OF *TAMBURLAINE*
## *THE GREAT*: PART TWO

### DRAMATIC CHARACTERS

**TAMBURLAINE:**   King of Persia and mighty lord of the world.

**CALYPHAS:**   Tamburlaine's son who is killed by his father because of his cowardice in refusing to fight.

**AMYRAS:**   Tamburlaine's son who is crowned his successor.

**CELEBINUS:**   Also a son of Tamburlaine.

**TECHELLES:**   King of Fez, one of Tamburlaine's leading generals.

**THERIDAMAS:**   King of Argier (Algiers). He woos Olympia.

**USUMCASANE:**   King of Morocco and a leader of Tamburlaine's forces.

**ORCANES:**   King of Natolia who is deceived by the Christians. He fights against Tamburlaine, but is defeated.

**KING OF JERUSALEM:** A prisoner of Tamburlaine's.

**KING OF TREBIZOND:** ⎫ Captives of Tamburlaine; they are
**KING OF SORIA:** ⎭ forced to draw his chariot.

**KING OF AMASIA:**    An ally of Callapine's against Tamburlaine.

**GAZELLUS:**    Viceroy of Byron; he fights with Orcanes against Tamburlaine.

**URIBASSA:**    Another lord of Asia who is an enemy of Tamburlaine.

**SIGISMUND:**    King of Hungary who deceives the Turks.

**FREDERICK:** ⎫ Lords of Buda and Bohemia who advise King
**BALDWIN:** ⎰ Sigismund to violate his oath to the Turks.

**CALLAPINE:**    Son of Bajazeth, who seeks revenge against Tamburlaine for his father's death.

**ALMEDA:**    Callapine's keeper in jail. He is bribed to let his prisoner escape, and he flees with Callapine.

**PERDICAS:**    Servant to Calyphas.

**GOVERNOR OF BABYLON:**    A brave ruler who defies Tamburlaine, but he is executed in cruel fashion.

**MAXIMUS:**    A citizen of Babylon.

**CAPTAIN OF BALSERA:**    Commander of a Turkish fortress.

**OLYMPIA:**    The captain's wife who resists Theridamas.

**HER SON:**    Killed by his mother to avoid Tamburlaine's cruelty.

**PHYSICIANS:**    Attend Tamburlaine at his death.

**ZENOCRATE:**    Tamburlaine's wife.

**OTHER CHARACTERS: LORDS, CITIZENS, SOLDIERS, ANOTHER CAPTAIN, TURKISH CONCUBINES.**

# TAMBURLAINE THE GREAT: PART II

## THE PROLOGUE

The general welcomes Tamburlaine received,
When he arrived last upon the stage,
Hath made our poet pen his Second Part,
Where death cuts off the progress of his pomp,
And murderous fates throw all his triumphs down.

## ACT I

Orcanes, King of Natolia, together with Gazellus, Viceroy of Byron, and Uribassa, all Turkish vassals of the defeated Bajazeth, decide that it is impossible to fight Tamburlaine in the East and the Christians in the West. And so they make peace with King Sigismund of Hungary in order that they may jointly face their common enemy in the East—Tamburlaine. Sigismund swears by Christ, and Orcanes swears by Mahomet, the Moslem god, to keep the peace. Callapine, Bajazeth's son and heir, escapes from Tamburlaine's prison by bribing his keeper Almeda with promises of great riches and a king's crown. Tamburlaine, now the father of three sons named Calyphus, Amyras, and Celebinus, complains that his sons are not warlike enough, and he demands that they strive to inherit kingship by noble feats of arms. Theridamas, King of Argier; Techelles, King of Fez; and Usumcasane, King of Morocco, tell Tamburlaine of their lengthy travels and extensive conquests, and they again pledge their allegiance to Tamburlaine.

## ACT II

Frederick, Lord of Buda, recalls to Sigismund former Christian losses to Turkish forces, and he also notes that much of the Turkish army has now been sent to meet Tamburlaine. Frederick advises Sigismund to attack the remaining pagan force now while the advantage is theirs. Baldwin, a lord of Bohemia, advances the theory that Christians are not bound to keep oaths made with pagans. Sigismund thus orders his forces to go out suddenly and attack the Turks. Orcanes, furious over the treachery of the Christians, calls upon the Christ whom the Christians have dishonored by breaking their vow to aid the Turks. The Turks are victorious, and Sigismund, acknowledging his "hateful perjury," dies calling upon Christ for "endless mercy." The Turks hasten then to join the kings of Jerusalem, Soria, Trebizond, and Amasia, and to fight against Tamburlaine. Meanwhile Zenocrate has become ill and she dies. Tamburlaine is infuriated by this loss: "Behold me here, divine Zenocrate,/ Raving, impatient, desperate, and mad. . . ." In his rage, Tamburlaine orders Zenocrate's body to be embalmed with cassia, ambergris, and myrrh: "Not lapt in lead, but in a sheet of gold,/ And till I die thou shalt not be interred." Thus Tamburlaine resolves to bear her body with him, and then he orders the city wherein she died to be consumed with fire.

## ACT III

The Kings of Trebizond, Soria, and Jerusalem, and Orcanes, King of Natolia, crown the escaped Callapine successor to his father Bajazeth as King of Turkey. Together they form a mighty host to fight Tamburlaine. Meanwhile Tamburlaine instructs his sons in the rudiments of war and stabs his own arm to show them his bravery. He bids his sons to wash their hands in his blood, and then orders them to fight nobly against the Turks. Techelles and Theridamas come with their armies to Balsera, a Turkish fortress. The Turkish Captain refuses to yield and is seriously wounded in the fray. In a touching scene, the Captain bids farewell before his death to his wife Olympia and their son. Olympia kills her son, burns her husband's and son's bodies and then prepares to kill herself in order to avoid the Scythian terror. But before she can stab herself, Theridamas and Techelles prevent her. Theridamas is so impressed by the beauty of Olympia that he tells her he is in love with her and that she must go with him. Techelles and Theridamas distribute the booty from their victory, and then march to meet Tamburlaine at Natolia for the attack on the Turks. The two armies gather at Aleppo, and at first spend the time exchanging threats and insults. Orcanes threatens that now the "scourge of Jove" will end his warlike progress. Tamburlaine warns the Turks that they shall so suffer that they shall curse the birth of Tamburlaine, and he says to Almeda, the jailor: "I'll make thee wish the earth had swallowed thee,/ See'st thou not death within my wrathful looks?" Orcanes crowns Almeda King of Ariadan.

## ACT IV

Calyphas, one of Tamburlaine's sons, refuses to join his brothers Amyras and Celebinus in the battle, and the Kings of Natolia, Trebizond, Jerusalem, and Soria are taken prisoners. Despite the pleas of his followers, Tamburlaine kills his son Calyphas: "Image of sloth and picture of a slave,/The obloquy and scorn of my renown!" He orders Turkish concubines to bury Calyphas, calling him "this effeminate brat," and then he gives the concubines to his common soldiers. Theridamas now continues his suit to Olympia, who prays for some means to end her life of grief. To end her thoughts of her husband and son, Theridamas promises Olympia great riches as Empress of Argier. When Theridamas tries to force himself upon Olympia, she gives him a magical ointment which prevents injury from any weapon. To prove the ointment's power, Olympia puts some on her neck and bids Theridamas strike at her throat. He does so and kills her. By this device Olympia gains release from her suffering. Meanwhile Tamburlaine further reveals his barbarity because he has the Kings of Trebizond and Soria—"ye pampered jades of Asia!"—with bits in their mouths draw his chariot to Babylon, the next object of his insatiable desire for conquest.

## ACT V

Maximus requests the Governor of Babylon to hang out flags of truce to mollify Tamburlaine's "intolerable wrath." Citizens also entreat the Governor to submit, but the Governor refuses to heed the pleas of these cowards. When Tamburlaine conquers the city, he orders the Governor to be hanged in chains from the city walls so that soldiers can shoot at him. Needing fresh "steeds" for his chariot, Tamburlaine orders the Kings of Natolia and Jerusalem to replace the kings of Trebizond and Soria. The Governor is seen hanging from the walls, and the soldiers shoot at him. Tamburlaine orders that all the people of Babylon are to be drowned in the city's lake. Then Tamburlaine commands that all copies of the Koran and other Turkish sacred books are to be burned. Callapine and the King of Amasia seek out Tamburlaine in the hope that they might defeat him. However, Tamburlaine has suddenly grown ill, and a map is brought to him so that he may trace his conquests. He entrusts the conquest of the rest of the world to his sons Amyras and Celebinus. Amyras is crowned Tamburlaine's successor. Zenocrate's hearse is brought in, and Tamburlaine, "the scourge of God," dies.

**COMMENT:** Marlowe wrote *Tamburlaine, Part II* as a result of the popular reception accorded *Tamburlaine, Part I*. *Tamburlaine, Part II* is largely Marlowe's own invention though he borrowed the Olympia-Theridamas episode from Ariosto's *Orlando Furioso,* and the perfidy of King Sigismund of Hungary in deceiving Orcanes and the Turks is based on historical facts leading to the battle of Varna in 1444. Marlowe's considerable learning and scholarship are revealed by his detailed knowledge of military fortifications, perhaps derived from Paul Ive's *The Practice of Fortification* published in 1589. Marlowe also used for the geography in both parts of *Tamburlaine* the *Theatrum Orbis Terrarum* of Abraham Ortelius, first published in Antwerp in 1570.

Where *Tamburlaine, Part I* focused upon the subjects of love and war, two themes Marlowe treated throughout his career, *Tamburlaine, Part II* is concerned with war and death. The same episodic structure, which reveals rather than develops Tamburlaine's character, is used again by Marlowe to impress upon us the greatness of the central figure. Three major war actions are undertaken: Turks versus Christians (Acts I and II), the Battle of Aleppo (Acts III and IV), and the siege of Babylon (Act V). The actions of King Sigismund reveal the treachery of Christians, but Sigismund is punished for his treachery because Orcanes and the Turks defeat Sigismund. Tamburlaine's victory in the Battle of Aleppo again reveals his cruelty, as he murders his shirking son Calyphas and then treats his prisoners like animals. After the siege of Babylon, Tamburlaine visits inhuman punishment upon the governor and orders all of the people to be drowned. These acts of barbarism continue the portrait of titanism from *Tamburlaine, Part I*.

However, death intrudes in *Tamburlaine II* to point up the mutability of earthly glory. Toward the end of *Tamburlaine, Part I*, Zenocrate, upon seeing the bodies of Bajazeth and Zabina, spoke of "slippery crowns" and of the fickleness of fortune. Now in *Tamburlaine, Part II* Zenocrate's death (Act II) becomes a grim reminder to the tyrant that though he be a scourge of God, he too is liable to death and an end of glory. Tamburlaine in his fury tries to overcome Zenocrate's death by carrying her hearse with him. It is Tamburlaine's fury and wrath that come to the fore in *Tamburlaine, Part II*, for his aspirations have reached the fantastic and the impossible. The preservation of Zenocrate's body ironically reveals the contrast between the reality of death and Tamburlaine's illusionary attempt to defy mortal limitations. At his own death Tamburlaine first asserts that death's fatal dart cannot wound him, and when he realizes that he cannot escpe death, Tamburlaine simply rages. Through titanic cruelty and violence Tamburlaine strives to transcend human limitations, but his outbursts simply produce in him the physical distress (cf. the First Physician's speech, Act V, Scene 3) which destroys him. Thus, in a sense, it is Tamburlaine's ambition which ironically impels him to his destruction.

The Sigismund-Orcanes plot in *Tamburlaine, Part I* provides an analogous action to the main plot because Orcanes calls upon Christ to punish the perfidy of Sigismund and the Christians. In contrast, when Tamburlaine burns the Koran and other Turkish sacred books, he calls upon Mahomet to work a miracle to save the books. The prayer to Mahomet, however, goes unanswered and the implication is that Mahomet is powerless. Sigismund, too, contrasts with Tamburlaine in death, for the King of Hungary meets death with repentance and Christian resignation. The Olympia-Theridamas sub-plot also contrasts with the main action, particularly with Tamburlaine's wooing and winning of Zenocrate in *Tamburlaine, Part I*. As a kind of *exempla,* Olympia, after her husband's death, kills her son, and then resists the overtures of Theridamas. Stoically and nobly Olympia kills herself rather than submit to her enemies. Tamburlaine's slaying of his cowardly son Calyphas also contrasts with the noble attitude of Olympia's son. These actions point up the limitation of human ambition and also of treachery and cruelty.

# BRIEF SUMMARY OF *THE JEW OF MALTA*

## DRAMATIC CHARACTERS

**FERNEZE:** The Christian Governor of Malta who confiscates Barabas's wealth to pay the Turkish tribute.

**LODOWICK:** Ferneze's son. He is a suitor to Abigail, but is the victim of Barabas's plot.

**SELIM CALYMATH:** Son of the Turkish Grand Seignior who comes to Malta to demand the tribute.

**MARTIN DEL BOSCO:** Vice-Admiral of Spain who encourages Christian resistance to the Turkish demand for tribute.

**MATHIAS:** A gentleman whom Abigail loves. However, he to is a victim of Barabas's cunning.

**BARABAS:** The Jew of Malta. A wealthy man who is expert in cunning, deceit, and revenge. He is a total villain.

**ITHAMORE:** Barabas's slave who hates Christians and practices villainy against them. He is the instrument to perform Barabas's plots.

**JACOMO:** A Friar who avariciously strives for wealth. He is executed for murder as a result of Barabas's intrigue.

**BARNARDINE:** The Friar who hears Abigail's confession. He is also one of Barabas's victims.

**PILIA-BORZA:**    A bully who aids Bellamira's blackmail plot against Barabas.

**THREE JEWS:**    Meekly surrender their wealth to Ferneze when he demands it.

**KATHERINE:**    Mother of Mathias.

**ABIGAIL:**    The saintly daughter of Barabas: his "jewel".

**BELLAMIRA:**    A courtesan of whom Ithamore is enamored. She blackmails Barabas.

**ABBESS:**    She is the head of the convent which receives Abigail.

**MACHIAVEL:**    Speaks the Prologue. He is the embodiment of the Elizabethan conception of Machiavellianism—villainy.

**OTHER CHARACTERS: TWO MERCHANTS, KNIGHTS, BASH-AWS, OFFICERS, GUARD, SLAVES, MESSENGER, CARPEN-TERS, NUN.**

**THE SCENE:**
Malta.

### THE JEW OF MALTA

### ACT I

Barabas, the Jew of Malta, sits in his counting-house admiring his heaps of gold when some merchants enter to report the safe arrival at Malta of several of the Jew's argosies. Barabas, in a soliloquy, then notes his own great wealth in contrast to the poverty of Christians in whose faith Barabas can see no fruits, "but malice, falsehood, and excessive pride. . . ."

Three Jews enter and call Barabas to an important meeting in the senate house. For years the Turks have held Malta under tribute, Barabas notes, but the Turks have let the tribute accumulate so that now not all the wealth of Malta could pay the tax. Calymath, son to the Grand Seignior of Turkey, demands the "ten years' tribute" in his father's name and allows Ferneze, the Governor of Malta, a month to collect it. Ferneze disallows Barabas's plea that the Jews are strangers (that is, not citizens) in Malta because they had leave to gather their wealth. Thus the Jews are to surrender one half of their estates; the penalty for refusal is forced conversion to Christianity, and if not this, then death. The three Jews agree to the terms quickly, and Barabas upbraids them for their cowardice. Barabas's reluctance results in Ferneze's decision to seize all of his wealth and not to allow him a chance to repent. Furthermore, the Christian rulers decide that Barabas's house is to be turned into a nunnery. Only Barabas receives this extreme punishment, and he rejects counsels to patience from his fellow Jews.

Barabas assures his grieving daughter that not all is lost because he has hidden ten thousand Portuguese gold coins, rich jewels, and precious stones under the floor of his house. Abigail, however, tells her father he will not be allowed to enter his home because nuns are there already and none but those of their sect may enter. Accordingly Barabas persuades his daughter to pretend conversion to Christianity and to seek entrance into the nunnery. Abigail meets the Abbess, and the Abbess agrees to accept her. As a part of his deceit, Barabas rushes in and accuses his daughter of deserting him:

> Child of perdition, and thy father's shame,
> What wilt thou do among these hateful fiends?
> I charge thee on my blessing that thou leave
> These devils and their damnèd heresy.

Whenever he has the chance, Barabas whispers to Abigail his instructions on how to get the gold. Mathias, a gentleman, and Lodowick, Ferneze's son, discuss Abigail's beauty and resolve to visit her.

## ACT II

At night Barabas comes to the nunnery, and Abigail throws down his gold. Meanwhile, Martin del Bosco, vice-admiral of Spain, arrives with his fleet at Malta and offers to sell some Turkish prisoners. At first Ferneze refuses to allow the sale because of the tributary league and debt of a hundred thousand crowns to Calymath, but Bosco reminds him of his obligation to resist the Turks. Ferneze, having received promise of Spanish military aid, decides to withold the tribute, resist the Turks, and allow Bosco's sale: "Honor is bought with blood and not with gold."

Barabas has bought a mansion to rival the Governor's palace, and when he meets Lodowick, Barabas encourages the young men's quest for a "diamond"—Abigail. At the sale of slaves, Barabas purchases Ithamore, who was born in Arabia: "Ay, mark him, you were best; for this is he/ That by my help shall do much villainy." Barabas instructs Ithamore, and boasts of his past to the slave:

> As for myself, I walk abroad' a nights
> And kill sick people groaning under walls.
> Sometimes I go about and poison wells,
> And now and then, to cherish Christian thieves,
> I am content to lose some of my crowns
> That I may, walking in my gallery,
> See 'em pinioned along by my door.

Ithamore tells Barabas of his hatred for Christians, and thus the two villains are united. When Lodowick comes to Barabas's house, he is welcomed and encouraged by Barabas in his suit for Abigail. Barabas orders Abigail to show favor to both young men because it is a part of his villainous plan. Abigail, however, sincerely loves Don Mathias. Barabas sows enmity between Lodowick and Mathias, and then he betroths Abigail to both of them. Abigail expresses displeasure at her father's actions, especially since they place her love for Mathias in danger. Barabas then sends Ithamore to Mathias with a forged challenge from Lodowick.

## ACT III

Bellamira, a courtesan, complains that her business has been slow since the city was besieged, and only Pilia-Borza, a bully, now comes. Pilia-Borza enters and tells Bellamira how he robbed a boy of silver from Barabas's counting-house. Ithamore passes and is struck by the beauty of the courtesan: "Now would I give a hundred of the Jew's crowns that I had such a concubine." As a result of the forged challenge, Lodowick and Mathias fight a duel in which they are both killed. When Ithamore discovers the success of his master's "bravest policy" to Abigail, she sends the slave for one of the friars at the new-made nunnery of St. Jacques. Confessing sincere resolve to become a Christian, Abigail is received into the nunnery by Friar Jacomo, Barabas, infuriated by Abigail's action, promises to make Ithamore his heir, and he orders Ithamore to bring a pot of rice porridge which he has poisoned to the nunnery. It is the Eve of St. Jacques, and it is the custom for all of Malta to send alms to the nunnery, and thus the porridge will find its way to Abigail. All of the nuns die, but Abigail confesses to Friar Barnadine her father's villainy and his responsibility for the deaths of Lodowick and Mathias. Abigail then dies a Christian.

The Turks now have returned to Malta for their tribute, but Ferneze refuses to pay, and the city prepares for attack.

## ACT IV

Friars Barnadine and Jacomo violate canon law and use the information gained from Abigail's confession to accuse Barabas of his crimes. Barabas, again dissembling, says that he wishes to become a Christian and offers great wealth to the friar who converts him. This appeal to the venality of the friars causes an argument between them. Barabas entertains the friars separately, and he and Ithamore strangle Friar Barnadine, who heard Abigail's confession. When Friar Jacomo comes to Barabas's house, he finds Friar Barnardine blocking his path because Barabas and Ithamore have set the corpse there. Jacomo, thinking Barnadine is attempting to prevent him from receiving the gold, strikes the body with a staff. Barabas and Ithamore seize Friar Jacomo and prepare to take him to court. Later summoned by a letter, Ithamore comes from the friar's hanging to Bellamira's house. Bellamira, the courtesan, entices Ithamore, who knows all of Barabas's secrets, to blackmail the Jew. While drunk, Ithamore confesses all Barabas's villainies to Bellamira and Pilia-Borza, who resolve to report the news to the Governor. But Barabas, disguised as a lute-player, visits Bellamira, Ithamore, and Pilia-Borza, and he poisons them all with a scented bouquet of flowers.

## ACT V

As the Governor prepares for war, Bellamira, Ithamore, and Pilia-Borza, before they die, bring forward their accusations against Barabas. Barabas feigns death by swallowing poppy and cold mandrake juice. After Ferneze has his body thrown over the city walls to be the prey of vultures and wild beasts. Barabas revives and offers aid to the Turks. Through this aid the Turks take Malta, and Barabas is made Governor. Barabas, realizing that he is hated by the people, and that he has no desire to rule, offers Ferneze a plot wherein for a hundred thousand pounds Barabas will regain the city for the Christians. Barabas invites Calymath to a banquet and offers him a richly prized pearl upon his coming. Calymath's soldiers are invited to banquet at a monastery outside the city walls, and Barabas has had explosives planted beneath the monastery. Barabas has also constructed a trap at the banquet which opens in the floor and hurls its victims into a boiling cauldron. Barabas says:

Why, is not this
A kingly kind of trade, to purchase towns
By treachery and sell 'em by deceit?
Now tell me, worldlings, underneath the sun
If greater falsehood ever has been done?

The monastery is blown up, but when the signal is given and the trap is sprung at the banquet, Barabas falls into the cauldron. At the last moment Ferneze decided to capture Calymath and the Turkish Bashaws alive and to punish Barabas for his villainy. Thus Barabas dies, and Malta has escaped capture by the Turks.

COMMENT:     Barabas in *The Jew of Malta* is a character with a definite relationship to the older Morality Vice. Indeed Barabas is not a character to be viewed from a realistic perspective because he is really a personification of vice and villainy. Three great mishaps befall Barabas during the play: his wealth is confiscated; his daughter Abigail converts to Christianity; and his servant Ithamore blackmails him. Initially Barabas, the Jew, is seen as a victim of Christian "policy," as Ferneze, the Governor of Malta, confiscates Barabas's wealth to pay the tribute to the Turks. Barabas reacts to this with hatred for the Christians and quickly he begins his intrigue to recover his gold. Wealth is Barabas's god, and his opening hymn to his gold reminds us of a later play: Jonson's *Volpone*. Gold becomes the central theme of the play, for Barabas, the Christians, and the Turks are all seeking it.

Abigail, Barabas's saintly daughter, is the instrument that Barabas uses to recover his weath. His affection for his daughter is based upon her value as a means to his wealth; he refers to her as his "diamond" when he talks to her suitors Mathias and Lodowick. Barabas says he loves Abigail as Agamemnon did Iphigeneia, and we recall the willingness of the Greek commander to sacrifice his daughter. Ironically, Barabas's use of Abigail in his plots results in her conversion to Christianity, and her final confession to Friar Barnardine is instrumental in undoing her father. Abigail, though, is the only thoroughly sympathetic creature in the play, and she embodies Christian perfection in its ideal sense. In the latter function she contrasts markedly with Ferneze and the Friars.

Ithamore, Barabas's servant, also "converts" from his master in that he joins the prostitute Bellamira in a blackmail plot against the Jew. Thus, the agent of his villainies seeks to take Barabas's wealth, but in the process Ithamore, Bellamira, and Pilia-Borza are murdered by the cunning Jew. Likewise Friars Jacomo and Barnardine are undone by Barabas's cunning when they contend for his wealth. Barabas is well-schooled in intrigue, dissimulation, revenge, poisons, and plots.

Barabas dominates *The Jew of Malta* and is another of Marlowe's "overreachers." As Jew, Barabas is the literal and figurative embodiment of greed, lack of faith, and worldliness; he is the embodiment of moral evil. Marlowe in the characterization of Barabas is of course presenting the common conception of what a Jew would be for the Elizabethans. The Elizabethan audience, when it saw Barabas poring over his gold in the opening scene, would immediately recognize him as a figure of avarice, and they would expect that as the play developed that it would confirm their identification of Jewishness with total villainy. In this sense, as a dramatic character Barabas should be compared with Shylock in Shakespeare's *The Merchant of Venice*. Barabas's name reminds us that Barabas was preferred to Christ when the people were asked who should go free. Thus, in *The Jew of Malta* Barabas is the antithesis of the Christian, and to choose or follow Barabas is to reject Christ. Barabas is also a Machiavellian intriguer, a man ready with the instrument of revenge, and a man possessing the will to effect his resolves. Machiavel speaks the Prologue to the play: "I count religion but a childish toy/ And hold there is no sin but ignorance." He is the personification of "policy" and the evils of Machiavellianism as described in Gentillet's *Contre Machiavel* (1576). *The Jew of Malta* disappoints many who feel that the final three acts are melodramatic and unworthy of the fine dramatic conception evident in the first two acts. When viewed from a "realistic" perspective, the characters certainly fade into flat abstractions, grotesque figures playing their parts in a sensationalist drama. No doubt the poisons. the duels, stabbings and explosions in *The Jew of Malta* are sensational, but if we allow for Barabas as being a kind of Morality Vice, then the play presents the ultimate undoing of evil and vice. Barabas, at the end, is the victim of his own intrigue, and the cauldron offered the Elizabethan audience a well-known symbol of punishment. Thus, in the end, Barabas, that inhuman monster, is the victim of a kind of poetic justice that demands the punishment of evil, but we as audience, recalling his horrible crimes, are in sympathy with the punishment Barabas receives.

# BRIEF SUMMARY OF *EDWARD THE SECOND*

## DRAMATIC CHARACTERS

**KING EDWARD THE SECOND:** King of England. A man by temper unfit to rule as he dotes upon flatterers such as Gaveston.

**PRINCE EDWARD:** The King's son who is later crowned Edward III.

**EARL OF KENT:** Brother of Edward the Second; he deserts the rebels in a desperate attempt to save his brother's life.

**GAVESTON:** The flattering favorite of the King who draws the ire and wrath of the rebellious nobles.

**WARWICK:** A lord opposed to Edward II. He has Gaveston executed.

**LANCASTER:** A noble lord in opposition to Edward II.

**PEMBROKE:** A rebel leader in charge of Gaveston while the latter is a prisoner.

**ARUNDEL:** A supporter of Edward II.

**LEICESTER:** He and his men capture Edward II at Neath.

**BERKELEY:** Sir Thomas of Berkeley, the gentle jailer of Edward II.

**MORTIMER SENIOR:** Edward II refuses to ransom him when he is captured by the Scots.

**MORTIMER JUNIOR:**    The most powerful of the rebels, he is initially a gallant opponent to the King's misrule. Later he becomes a scheming and ambitious villain. Protector of the realm under Edward III.

**SPENCER SENIOR:**    A war-like follower of the King.

**SPENCER JUNIOR:**    His son; a former servant of the Earl of Gloucester; he replaces Gaveston in the King's favor.

**ARCHBISHOP OF CANTERBURY:**    Takes part in the demand for the banishment of Gaveston. Later he crowns Edward III.

**BISHOP OF COVENTRY:**    Gaveston in revenge for his former exile orders the seizure of the Bishop's holdings.

**BISHOP OF WINCHESTER:**    The church's witness at the deposition of Edward II.

**BALDOCK:**    A former scholar in the service of the Earl of Gloucester. He becomes one of Edward's favorites.

**BEAUMONT:**    Edward II's messenger.

**GURNEY:**    These two villains are in the hire of Mortimer.
**MATREVIS:**    They torture Edward II in prison.

**LIGHTBORN:**    A murderer hired by Mortimer to kill Edward II; he is killed by Gurney and Matrevis.

**SIR JOHN OF HAINAULT:** He befriends Isabella while she is in France.

**LEVUNE:**    A French diplomat who is bribed to prevent Isabella's success in France.

**QUEEN ISABELLA:**    At first the devoted wife of Edward II, she later joins the rebels. She falls in love with Mortimer.

**NIECE TO EDWARD II:**    Daughter of the Earl of Gloucester and betrothed to Gaveston.

**OTHER CHARACTERS: TRUSSEL, RICE AP HOWELL, ABBOT, MONKS, HERALDS, LORDS, POOR MEN, MOWER, CHAMPION, MESSENGERS, SOLDIERS, ATTENDANTS, LADIES.**

**THE SCENE:**    England, France.

# EDWARD THE SECOND

## ACT I

Pierce Gaveston has been recalled from his exile in France by the newly crowned King Edward II, who has succeeded to the throne at the death of his father Edward I. Edward's invitation to Gaveston greatly pleases Gaveston because he will now share the kingdom with his friend. Gaveston plans to draw "the pliant king" with music, masques, wanton poetry, and pleasing shows. The Barons and Earls openly proclaim to the King their opposition to Gaveston's return, but the King wilfully rejects their protests. Mortimer Senior, Mortimer Junior, Lancaster, and Warwick warn the King of oaths to Edward I to prevent Gaveston's return and further that they will not aid him when he needs them. Lancaster says:

> Adieu, my lord, and either change your mind,
> Or look to see the throne, where you should sit,
> To float in blood, and at thy wanton head
> The glozing head of thy base minion thrown.

However, Edward creates Gaveston Lord High Chamberlain, Chief Secretary of State, Earl of Cornwall, King and Lord of the Isle of Man, and furthermore he gives Gaveston power to command as he pleases. Gaveston immediately has the Bishop of Coventry, who was responsible for his exile, thrown into prison, and he confiscates his house and goods. The Mortimers, Lancaster, and Warwick are furious over Gaveston's new titles, and the Archbishop of Canterbury, angered by the fate of Coventry, joins the nobles in their demands that Gaveston be banished again. Queen Isabella, Edward's wife, complains to the lords of her husband's inattention to her and of his excessive doting upon his favorite—Gaveston. The Archbishop of Canterbury proposes that they gather at the New Temple to confirm Gaveston's banishment. Much against his will, Edward is forced to subscribe to the order banishing Gaveston. Despite Gaveston's remarks on her honor and her friendship with Mortimer, Isabella takes pity on the King's desperate grief at the loss of his favorite. Edward banishes Isabella from his sight, and Isabella, hoping to regain favor with her husband, resolves to try to obtain Gaveston's recall. The younger Mortimer, indicating that Gaveston can be murdered when he returns to England, prevails with the lords, and the banishment is repealed. Edward is overjoyed at this turn of events, receives Isabella again, and then announces that he has betrothed his niece, the daughter of the Earl of Gloucester, to Gaveston.

## ACT II

The recent death of the Earl of Gloucester forces two of his former servants, Spencer Junior and Baldock the scholar, to seek new employment. Aware of Gaveston's recall and of his betrothal to the Earl of Gloucester's daughter, they both decide to serve Gaveston. Both are very capable of hypocrisy, and they know that serving Gaveston will gain them proximity to the King. While at Tynemouth awaiting Gaveston's arrival, Mortimer Junior and Lancaster describe to the King the satiric emblems on their shields. Both devices warn that Gaveston is a deadly canker to the King. When Gaveston arrives, the lords insult him and threaten his life. Mortimer Junior wounds Gaveston in a fracas. Open rebellion erupts when the King refuses to ransom Mortimer Senior who has been captured by the Scots while fighting in Edward's behalf. The lords point out the dissolute and spendthrift nature of Edward's rule as the cause for their rebellion, and they attack Gaveston at Tynemouth and pursue him to Scarborough. Queen Isabella at this point decides to importune Edward's love once again, and if she fails, then she will go to France with her son to complain to her brother, the King of France. Meanwhile Gaveston is taken prisoner, and the King requests the lords that he be allowed to see Gaveston one more time. The King's request is granted over Warwick's heated opposition. Gaveston is left in the keeping of the Earl of Pembroke prior to the meeting with the King. Pembroke, however, leaves Gaveston with his servant James while he goes to visit his wife at their home nearby.

## ACT III

Warwick seizes Gaveston from James and the Earl of Pembroke's men and executes him. Edward, now aided by Spencer Senior and having Spencer Junior as a new favorite, swears vengeance upon the barons. The barons send a messenger to the King demanding that he give up the pernicious upstart Spencer Junior and other such dissembling flatterers. Edward is victorious in battle against the barons, and Kent, the King's brother, along with Warwick, Lancaster, and Young Mortimer are taken prisoners. Warwick and Lancaster are executed, Mortimer is imprisoned in the Tower, and Kent is banished.

While all this is happening, the French have seized English territory in Normandy, and Edward sends Isabella and Prince Edward, their son, to parley with the King of France. However,

Spencer Junior bribes Levune, a French diplomat, to make sure that Isabella's pleas fall on deaf ears in France.

## ACT IV

Aided by Kent, Mortimer Junior drugs his guards and escapes from his prison in the Tower. Mortimer and Kent sail for France to join Queen Isabella and Prince Edward who have found no help from the French King. Sir John of Hainault befriends Isabella in her distress and aids her and the newly arrived nobles, Kent and Mortimer, with their plans to return to England. News arrives in England of these doings via a letter from Levune to Spencer Junior, now Earl of Gloucester, and Edward prepares to meet the rebel forces in the field. Isabella now turns her affections to the younger Mortimer, and together they defeat the King of Bristol. Spencer Senior is captured, and reports come in that Edward, Spencer Junior, and Baldock have escaped to Ireland. But Edward, Spencer Junior, and Baldock are unable to reach Ireland and instead disguise themselves and take refuge in a monastery. However, a mower, "a gloomy fellow in a mead below," spots them and leads the Earl of Leicester to their hideout where they are captured.

## ACT V

King Edward at Kenilworth Castle, Leicester's seat, is forced to abdicate. At this point Edward is a figure of considerable pathos, if not of tragic grandeur, for he is a man more sinned against than sinning. By Isabella's order, King Edward is given over to the charge of Sir Thomas Berkeley. Upon hearing of the gentleness of Berkeley, Mortimer Junior summons Gurney and Matrevis, two villains, whom he puts in charge of the King, and Mortimer orders them to shift the King back and forth from Berkeley Castle to Killingworth and to treat him bitterly. The King's new keepers treat him mercilessly as they starve him and shave his beard in puddle water. Edmund, Earl of

Kent and brother to the King, repents of his former allegiance with Mortimer and attempts to rescue Edward at Killingworth; however, Kent is captured by the guards and brought to court. Mortimer, meanwhile, recognizes that sympathy for the deposed monarch is growing among the commons, and thus he issues a riddling order calling for Edward's death. It reads:

> *Edwardum occidere nolite timere bonum est;*
> Fear not to kill the king, tis good to die.
> But read it thus, and that's another sense:
> *Edwardum occidere nolite timere bonum est;*
> Kill not the King, tis good to fear the worst.
> Unpointed as it is, thus shall it go,
> That, being dead, if it chance to be found,
> Matrevis and the rest may bear the blame,
> And we quit that caused it to be done.

Unpunctuated ("unpointed") or with a comma before the last two words, the Latin gives a command for murder. But if it is unpunctuated, or if the comma is before the last three words, it is a prohibition against murder. The lack of punctuation causes confusion. Mortimer summons his murderer, Lightborn, who is to carry the message and perform the deed. Unknowingly Lightborn also bears instructions for his own murder after the King has been killed. Mortimer, now acting as the Prince's protector, takes great comfort in his position and feels that he is the master of fortune: "The Prince I rule, the Queen do I Command. . . ." Prince Edward is crowned King Edward III, but when he intervenes in his uncle's behalf, he is overruled by the Lord Protector, Mortimer, who orders Kent executed. When Lightborn enters Edward's dungeon, he feigns pity at the horrible condition of the King who has been starved, kept from sleep, and been forced to live in a filthy dungeon. Lightborn persuades the King to rest on a bed of feathers, and at a signal Matrevis and Gurney rush in with a table which is placed on top of Edward. They all stamp on the table, and thus kill the king. Gurney then stabs Lightborn. King Edward III is horrified by news of his father's death, and he takes action

quickly by seizing Mortimer and orders that Mortimer be be-
headed for his crimes. Mortimer faces death with resignation:

> Base Fortune, now I see that in thy wheel
> There is a point, to which when men aspire,
> They tumble headlong down. That point I touched,
> And, seeing there was no place to mount up higher,
> Why should I grieve at my declining fall?
> Farewell, fair Queen; weep not for Mortimer,
> That scorns the world, and, as a traveller,
> Goes to discover countries yet unknown.

King Edward III orders his mother, Queen Isabella, imprisoned
in the Tower until further trial be made of her guilt.

**COMMENT:** Marlowe went to Raphael Holinshed's *Chronicles of England, Scotland, and Ireland* (1577; 1587) for most
of the historical material in Edward II, which covers the years
from the coronation of Edward II in 1307 to the execution of
Mortimer in 1330. Holinshed's *Chronicles,* it should be noted,
served as Shakespeare's major source for his history plays,
and Shakespeare's Henry VI plays preceded Marlowe's *Edward II.* This last fact makes for an interesting comparison because Marlowe, unlike Shakespeare, focuses more on personal
and individual suffering in his play than on the historical and
national problems. Other sources used by Marlowe for Edward
II include Robert Fabyan's *New Chronicles of England and
France,* John Stow's *Summary of English Chronicles,* and
Thomas Churchyard's "The Two Mortimer's" in the 1578
edition of *A Mirror for Magistrates.*

Elizabethan dramatists in the 1590's turned to the writing
of history plays in part because of the aroused sense of national-
ism consequent to such glorious achievements as the defeat
of the Spanish Armada in 1588. Elizabeth in her reign em-
bodied the fulfillment of the Tudor myth, which prophesied
the return of the ancient Arthurian line to the throne, and
the consequent end to civil war and bloodshed in regard to
rightful occupancy and succession to the throne. Under the

enduring and popular reign of Elizabeth, England truly achieved a kind of "golden age." The War of the Roses between the Houses of Lancaster and York, which preceded the Tudor reign, were recalled in Shakespeare's histories (*e.g., Richard II, Henry IV, Parts I* and *II*) and offered audiences grim reminders of civil bloodshed. But these plays emphasized the Tudor settlement and also offered a sense of the coming glory of England. They gave to the people a renewed sense of national pride. History, furthermore, offered the dramatist a ready-made "realistic" plot, and the stories of Kings often readily fitted the pattern of *de casibus* tragedy: the fall of a great man from a high position. Where Shakespeare was largely concerned with such problems as the divine right of kings, Marlowe in different fashion in *Edward II* is concerned with the fall of a weak man, a man, though, who was King of England.

Edward II presents the portrait of a king who totally disregards kingship to satisfy his personal desires and wanton passions. Edward is the pathetic victim of personal weaknesses, and his affection for the scheming flatterer Gaveston is an unnatural one. There is an obvious strain of homosexuality in the relationship, as may be seen from Gaveston's use of erotic language in his opening speech wherein he talks of Edward's letter recalling him to England:

> What greater bliss can hap to Gaveston
> Than live and be the favorite of a king?
> Sweet prince, I come; these thy amorous lines
> Might have enforced me to have swum from France,
> And, like Leander, gasped upon the sand,
> So thou wouldst smile and take me in thy arms.

Gaveston's reference to Leander, who swam the Hellespont to see his beloved Hero, indicates the unnatural love of Edward and Gaveston. Lacking in the personal and public virtues necessary for kingship, Edward expends himself upon his dissolute concern for the well-being of Gaveston. The opposition of the nobles and their rebellion initially offers the voice of the commonweal crying out against improper rule. Edward also rejects his wife, Isabella, who in her personal isolation parallels the disregard in which Edward holds the nation. Throughout the first three acts our sympathies are with Mortimer Junior, Isabella, and the rebellious lords, for they embody a sense of concern for the health of England Edward's weakness, his inattention to everything but Gaveston, and his abuse of authority remove the possibility of sympathy. Try as he may, however, Edward cannot achieve the isolation he desires, and he is deprived of his minion by Warwick. But Edward then adopts Spencer Junior and Baldock as his new flattering favorites.

The last two acts, however, bring a marked shift of sympathies. After his capture and imprisonment, Edward becomes increasingly concerned for his crown and he speaks consistently of his kingship:

> The griefs of private men are soon allayed,
> But not of kings. The forest deer, being struck,
> Runs to an herb that closeth up the wounds,
> But when the imperial lion's flesh is gored,
> He rends and tears it with his wrathful paw,
> And highly scorning that the lowly earth
> Should drink his blood, mounts up into the air.
> And so it fares with me, whose dauntless mind
> The ambitious Mortimer would seek to curb,
> And that unnatural queen, false Isabel,
> That thus hath pent and mewed me in a prison;
> For such outrageous passions cloy my soul,
> As with the wings of rancor and disdain
> Full often am I soaring up to heaven,
> To plain me to the gods against them both.

In the final acts of the play Marlowe presents Edward as a pathetic figure whose sufferings evoke sympathy for him. Lack of sympathy was caused earlier because we were aware that Edward's personal weaknesses were at the expense of his kingship. Now that very kingship in the final acts again commands our sympathies because we see its representative treated so foully. Also now the rebels, Isabella and Mortimer, become the embodiments of personal weakness. Mortimer, who earlier possessed the valor and nobility of a Hotspur (Shakespeare's *Henry IV, Part* I), now schemes to murder the King. Mortimer's instruments are Gurney and Matrevis, two villains who subject the King to inhuman sufferings. Lightborn, who is hired by Mortimer to kill Edward, reminds us of Barabas in *The Jew Of Malta* because, like the Morality Vice, he is a personification of evil. Lightborn's dissimulation wherein he feigns sympathy for Edward's condition before he murders him is the last grim deception that reveals the villainy of Mortimer. Mortimer's love for Isabella, his conduct as Lord Protector, and his order for the execution of Kent all reveal instances of the personal evils which alienate our sympathies. Like Kent, who left the rebels and desperately tried to save his brother King Edward, our sympathies shift in the course of the play. At the end it is the office of King that we see suffering and for which we sympathize. Edward's constant references to his crown, to the glory of his office, to his present condition in contrast to the past present to us a figure who has been laid low by his own failures and the villainy and ambition of others:

> And there in mire and puddle have I stood
> This ten days' space; and, lest that I should sleep,
> One plays continually upon a drum.
> They give me bread and water, being a king;
> So that, for want of sleep and sustenance,
> My mind's distempered, and my body's numbed,
> And whether I have limbs or no I know not.
> O, would my blood dropped out from every vein,
> As doth this water from my tattered robes.
> Tell Isabel, the Queen, I looked not thus,
> When for her sake I ran at tilt in France
> And there unhorsed the Duke of Cleremont.

*Edward II,* then, presents to us the tragedy of a man who was a failure because of personal weaknesses. In *Doctor Faustus* Marlowe portrays the tragedy of the man who aspires to go beyond human limitations; here in *Edward II* he presents the tragedy of a man who fails to realize his greatness, who fails to become a true king. At the end of *Edward II* villainy (Isabella and Mortimer) is punished, and order is restored in the reign of Edward III; but there is a loss too.

The major action of *Edward II*, following the *de casibus* pattern, presents the fall of a man from high place to wretchedness; King Edward is toppled from his throne to stand in mire and a puddle, and to meet death at the hand of a hired assassin. Edward's references to his crown and to his past glory, his pathetic pleas to be recognized as King of England, and his anguished cries of self-pity are of no avail. The mower who betrays the King when he seeks protection at Neath in the monastery, may well have carried a scythe on stage, and in this character the audience would have quickly recognized the grim reaper—time, death.

# SAMPLE QUESTIONS AND ANSWERS

1. What is the importance of Faustus's opening speech in Act I, Scene 1?

**ANSWER:** Faustus, in his opening speech, reviews the courses of study—philosophy, medicine, law, theology—open to human inquiry. However, Faustus has mastered all these studies, and he finds them too "servile" and "illiberal." Such studies do not free Faustus, and he is intent on pursuing something beyond the ordinary course of study. He finds that he is limited by the fact that he is still but a man, and he wishes that through medicine he might make men live eternally, or raise the dead to life again. Faustus implicitly draws an analogy here to the power of Christ, whose sacrifice brought eternal life to man and who also raised Lazarus from the dead. These lines reveal Faustus's ambition and his pride, for he would be like God. His sin is that of Lucifer: pride.

When Faustus discusses divinity, he reads from Jerome's Bible that the reward of sin is death, and after constructing a fallacious syllogism, Faustus concludes that what will be, shall be. In these lines, we see the introduction of one of the play's controlling ironies because what Faustus wills, shall be. His choice is to reject God and to pursue cursed necromancy, and this choice leads to the inevitable reward of sin, the spiritual death of Faustus's soul. Also in this speech we see Faustus imagining the vast powers that will be his as a result of his study of magic. The tremendous difference between Faustus's grand designs and their vacuous fulfillment is another major irony of the play.

Dramatically this opening speech indicates Faustus's great

learning to the audience, and it serves to introduce Faustus's choice and the reason for it.

2. What is the dramatic function of the Good and Bad Angels?

**ANSWER:**     Marlowe's *Doctor Faustus* in its use of the personified Good and Bad Angels reveals the influence of the older morality play tradition. Morality drama was allegorical and didactic, and usually dealt with the struggle of an Everyman-type figure against the forces of evil represented frequently by the Seven Deadly Sins. Man's victory emphasized the positive forces of grace and a life following religious and ethical teachings. The negative aspect, or man's defeat, was the reverse of this movement, and dramatists found this appealing because it offered the moral lesson that retributive justice punished sin. Obviously, there is a close relationship between tragedy and this latter process, and *Doctor Faustus* is a type of reverse morality play because it is concerned with spiritual defeat and not victory.

In *Doctor Faustus* the Good and Bad Angel, as in the morality play, contend for Faustus's soul. They represent in an exterior way the interior conflict of Faustus between good and evil. The Good and Bad Angel appear repeatedly throughout the play to show the recurring torment within Faustus's soul. The Good Angel signifies the presence of grace and repeatedly urges Faustus to repent. The Bad Angel represents evil and the forces leading Faustus to damnation. Dramatically, these personified figures offered Marlowe a way, other than the soliloquy, to present Faustus's spiritual struggle.

3. What is the dramatic function of the comic scenes in *Doctor Faustus?*

**ANSWER:**     The comic scenes in *Doctor Faustus* have been taken by some critics to be later additions with no bearing on the central meaning of the play. This attitude looks upon the comic scenes as unfortunate intrusions into the major serious action. Though the scenes may have been written by a collaborator named Samuel Rowley, we may suspect that Marlowe shaped the overall plans and allowed for the comic scenes. At any rate, we have to deal with the play as we have it, and this means taking the comic scenes as part of the play. No doubt, the comic portions were entertaining and provided lively theater for the audience. However, the larger question is one of whether these scenes are in any way related to the theme and meaning of *Doctor Faustus*. The answer is yes when we look at the Wagner conjuring scene as a parody of the major action of the play. The comic sub-plot mirrors on a different plane the serious action of the main plot, and it reveals how Faustus's magical powers are available to lesser types. The comic scenes, showing Faustus as a practical joker slapping the Pope's face and cheating the Horse-Courser, are also integrally related to the play's meaning because they ironically reveal the contrast between Faustus's visions of magical power and the ludicrous reality of his magic at work.

4. Discuss the significance of Faustus's contract with Lucifer in Act II, Scene I and his renewal of the contract in Act V, Scene One.

**ANSWER:** Faustus makes his contract with Lucifer by stabbing his arm and sealing the contract with his own blood. When Faustus says "It is finished," he repeats the words of Christ on the cross. Faustus's blasphemy is the verbal equivalent of the action he has just taken, for he has rejected God and delivered his soul to Lucifer. His fear of the devils overwhelms any thoughts of repentance, and Mephistophilis gives him a dagger and counsels despair. When Mephistophilis threatens Faustus because of his disobedience to Lucifer, Faustus repents for thinking of Christ's mercy, asks Lucifer's pardon, and then confirms again his former vow. Faustus here parodies the three stages of Christian penance (contrition, confession, satisfaction). These two scenes, then, illustrate the nature of Faustus's contract, and the parodying of religious language and ritual vividly conveys the blasphemy which Faustus commits.

5. What dramatic purpose does the Chorus serve?

**ANSWER:** The Chorus speaks before Acts I, III, and IV,

and delivers the Epilogue at the end. The Prologue to Act I gives the exposition of the narrative material needed by the audience to understand the subsequent action. In the Prologue, the Chorus narrates Faustus's biography, compares him to Icarus, and foreshadows Faustus's death. The Prologue, then, really gives a summary of the entire play, and as we watch the play we anxiously anticipate the fulfillment of what the Prologue has announced. The Prologue to Act III narrates the fabulous journeys of Faustus and gives us narrative material which Marlowe could not present dramatically. Here the Chorus is a conventional shorthand device which enables the dramatist to narrate rather than show by dramatic action. The Prologue to Act III tells us what Faustus has done before he came to Rome in Act III. The Prologue to Act IV does much the same thing because it introduces us to Faustus at the time of his return to Germany and the Court of the Emperor. As Epilogue the Chorus provides the conventional moral comment on the action of the play.

6. Discuss the role of the Old Man in Act V.

**ANSWER:**　　　The Old Man in Act V appeals to Faustus to leave his damned art and to ask God's forgiveness. In many particulars, the Old Man is like the Good Angel because his counsel to Faustus is the same. He takes on many of the qualities of a morality personification, perhaps something like Good Counsel. After the Faustus-Helen episode, the Old Man is aware that Faustus has completely damned himself. The Old Man is then tried by Satan, but his faith prevails against the devils and hell. Thus the Old Man achieves a spiritual victory, and dramatically this contrasts with Faustus's choice of evil and his ultimate damnation. Marlowe, through the Old Man, shows that the temptation to evil may be resisted and that spiritual victory can be achieved.

7. Discuss the structure of *Doctor Faustus*.

**ANSWER:**　　　Doctor Faustus contains a major pattern of action which deals with Faustus's choice to follow magic and to sell his soul to Lucifer. A comic plot, probably written by a collaborator, comments on and parodies the serious action of the main plot. Structurally, the play may be described as episodic because Marlowe gives us a series of actions which repeats the struggle of Faustus between the choice of God or Lucifer. Thus the recurrence of Good and Bad Angels, the repeated thoughts of repentance, and the appearance of the Old Man in Act V indicate the episodic and repetitive pattern of the play's structure. The comic portions of the play illustrate by irony the vacuous accomplishments consequent to Faustus's bargain. Wagner's conjuring and later Robin and Dick's ability at magic are parodies of Faustus's ability. By way of contrast the comic scenes serve to point up the terrible nature of Faustus's bargain, for these scenes reveal that the powers of magic are not nearly so great as Faustus imagined. Marlowe, then, by repeating the basic struggle of good and evil, structures his play so that the cumulative effect reveals the turmoil in Faustus's soul and produces awe and wonder at his tragic fall.

8. Indicate one of the major themes of *Tamburlaine, Parts I & II*.

**ANSWER:** *Tamburlaine, Part I* traces the rise of Tamburlaine from Scythian shepherd to mighty lord of the world. In this play we again meet a characteristic Marlovian hero—a man aspiring to greatness. Tamburlaine's heroic quest for power is accompanied by deeds of extraordinary cruelty, such as the inhuman treatment of Bajazeth and Zabina in Part I. The dream of empire expressed by Tamburlaine in lofty flights of hyperbole and bombastic rhetoric is matched by the superhuman energy and might of the conqueror. Marlowe in *Tamburlaine, Part I* presents, then, the rise of the great man to eminence, a rise accomplished without regard for the nature of the means. Everything must submit to Tamburlaine's dream of "perfect bliss," which is the possession of an earthly crown.

*Tamburlaine, Part II* continues the mighty conquests of Tamburlaine, but in this play Tamburlaine meets his end. The death of Zenocrate is a crushing blow to him, and he rages against it. Tamburlaine now is brought face to face with powers that he cannot control; he is made terribly aware of human limitation. Unable to cope with these facts, Tamburlaine is driven to the extremes of rage and continued cruelty. His death signifies the end of earthly ambition. Thus, the theme of ambition, of human aspiration for earthly glory and power, is seen confined by death. Though Tamburlaine's deeds are mighty, and though his dreams are great, yet he is a victim of death. This theme and pattern of action in *Tamburlaine, Part II* reveal a close adherence to the rise and fall of heroes pattern seen in much of Elizabethan tragedy.

9. Discuss the role of Ithamore in *The Jew of Malta*.

**ANSWER:** Ithamore, a slave, becomes the servant of Barabas and is the tool of his hate and vengeance. Ithamore brings his own hatred of Christians to assist Barabas in his revenge plot against the Christians for depriving him of his wealth and his daughter Abigail. Barabas is a kind of Machiavellian figure given to extraordinary intrigues, ingenious methods of torture, and secretive poisoning techniques. Ithamore is his ally in all of this, and he brings to the play, along with Barabas, many of the features of the Morality Vice. Of course, it is Ithamore's attraction for the prostitute Bellamira that leads in part to Barabas's downfall. When Ithamore leaves Barabas, it is the third great loss for Barabas in the play. Gold is at the heart of this defection because Bellamira blackmails Barabas with the information extracted from Ithamore. However, Barabas is too cunning for the villainous slave, and, with the aid of a disguise, Barabas poisons Ithamore, Bellamira, and Pilia-Borza with a scented bouquet of flowers. This act of dissimulation further links Barabas with one of the characteristic actions of the morality vice.

10. How does Edward II affect us as a dramatic character?

**ANSWER:** Throughout the first half of Edward II our sympathies are with the rebels who are opposed to the weak and dissolute reign of Edward II. The rebels, Mortimer, Lancaster, and Warwick, appeal to the office of king and Edward's total neglect of that office as the reason for their rebellion.

Edward's unnatural affection for his flattering sycophant, Gaveston, is the major issue of contention. Thus, because of our awareness of and respect for what a king should be, we are hostile to Edward throughout the first half of the play. In the final acts of *Edward II,* Edward takes on pathetic stature, if not tragic grandeur. Marlowe succeeds here in presenting a character whose suffering and anguish are truly human, something to which we can readily respond. Edward's repeated references to kingship, his crown, and the glory that should be his, remind us constantly that he is King of England. The inhuman sufferings that he is forced to undergo also call forth sympathy. Meanwhile the rebels, particularly Mortimer and Isabella, alienate our sympathies because they now resort to personal viciousness, intrigue, and villainy. Mortimer's use of Gurney, Matrevis, and Lightborn testifies to his ambitious nature.

In conclusion, our sympathies are engaged at the end for Edward because of our respect for his office and because of our horror at his suffering. Marlowe, then, accomplishes much the same thing that Shakespeare does later in *Richard II.*

# SUBJECT BIBLIOGRAPHY AND GUIDE
# TO RESEARCH PAPERS

## EDITIONS

The standard scholarly edition of *Doctor Faustus* is that edited by W. W. Greg: *Marlowe's "Doctor Faustus" 1604-1616* (1950). Greg's edition prints the A and B texts and is invaluable for scholarly work. The recent edition in The Revels Plays series, *Doctor Faustus,* ed. John D. Jump (1962), is an excellent scholarly edition which contains a perceptive and informative introduction. The appendix to this edition contains portions of the A text and of Marlowe's source, *The Damnable Life. The Complete Plays of Christopher Marlowe* (1963), edited by Irving R. Ribner, is a well printed, readable one volume edition with an informative critical introduction. Professor Ribner, however, hews closely to the line that Marlowe's plays reveal his personal "agnosticism." *Christopher Marlowe (Five Plays)*, ed. Havelock Ellis (1956; paperback), though not as scholarly as the other editions, is worth the price. It includes *Tamburlaine I & II, Doctor Faustus, The Jew of Malta,* and *Edward II.*

## CRITICAL READINGS ON MARLOWE'S BACKGROUND, LIFE, AND WORKS

BAKER, HOWARD. *An Induction to Tragedy* (1939). An important study that questions Senecan influence on English drama. Excellent for background to Marlowe's tragedies.

BAKELESS, JOHN. *Christopher Marlowe* (1937). Extremely valuable.

BATTENHOUSE, ROY W. *Marlowe's Tamburlaine: A Study in Renaissance Moral Philosophy* (1941). A learned, scholarly, and authoritative book, though it tends to view Marlowe's plays "too morally."

BEVINGTON, DAVID M. *From Mankind to Marlowe: Growth of Structure in the Popular Drama of Tudor England* (1962). An important study of the contribution of native elements to structure.

BLUESTONE, MAX and RABKIN, NORMAN, eds. *Shakespeare's Contemporaries* (1961). Includes critical essays on Marlowe.

BOAS, FREDERICK S. *An Introduction to Tudor Drama* (1933). A critical survey of sixteenth-century drama; contains a chapter on Marlowe.

BOAS, FREDERICK S. *Christopher Marlowe: A Biographical and Critical Study* (1940). A standard scholarly reference.

BOWERS, FREDSON THAYER. *Elizabethan Revenge Tragedy: 1587-1642* (1940). The standard study of a major Elizabethan dramatic convention.

BOYER, CLARENCE VALENTINE. *The Villain as Hero in Elizabethan Tragedy* (1914). Contains perceptive comment on *The Jew of Malta*.

BRADBROOK, MURIEL C. *Themes and Conventions of Elizabethan Tragedy* (1960; paperback). Contains a good chapter on Marlowe.

BROOKE, C. F. TUCKER. *The Tudor Drama* (1911). Still a valuable critical survey of English drama from its medieval origins to Marlowe's time.

BUTLER, E. M. *The Fortunes of Faust* (1952). Study of the Faust myth; its origins and development.

CAMPBELL, LILY B. *"Doctor Faustus*: A Case of Conscience," *PMLA,* LXVII (1952), 219-239.

COLE, DOUGLAS. *Suffering and Evil in the Plays of Christopher Marlowe* (1962). Emphasis is on Marlowe's theological learning. One of the finest critical studies to appear on Marlowe.

ECCLES, MARK. *Christopher Marlowe in London* (1934). Studies Marlowe's relationship to Thomas Watson.

ELIOT, T. S. *Essays on Elizabethan Drama* (1956; paperback). Mr. Eliot makes some stimulating comments about Marlowe's blank verse and about *The Jew of Malta* as "farce."

ELLIS-FERMOR, U. M. *Christopher Marlowe* (1927).

FARNHAM, WILLARD. *The Medieval Heritage of Elizabethan Tragedy* (1936). A landmark in scholarship; excellent for Marlowe's background.

GARDNER, HELEN. "Milton's 'Satan' and the Theme of Damnation," *English Studies*, n.s., I (1948), 46-66.


GREG, W. W. "The Damnation of Faustus," *MLR,* XLI (1946), 97-107.


HENDERSON, PHILIP. *Christopher Marlowe* (1956). A study of Marlowe's life and works.


HOTSON, J. LESLIE. *The Death of Christopher Marlowe* (1925). A piece of detective work that gave us the facts on Marlowe's death.


KAUFMAN, RALPH J., ed. *Elizabethan Drama: Modern Essays in Criticism* (1961).


KOCHER, PAUL H. *Christopher Marlowe: A Study of His Thought, Learning, Character* (1946). Stresses Marlowe's life in relation to his plays.


LEECH, CLIFFORD, ed. *Marlowe: A Collection of Critical Essays* (1964).


LEVIN, HARRY. *The Overreacher: A Study of Christopher Marlowe* (1952). An invaluable study treating the Marlovian tragic hero as the singular man. Levin relates the plays closely to Marlowe's life.


MAXWELL, J. C. "The Plays of Christopher Marlowe," in *The Age of Shakespeare,* vol. II, *The Pelican Guide to English Literature,* ed. Boris Ford (rev. ed. 1962). A general survey.

MC COLLUM, WILLIAM G. *Tragedy* (1957). An excellent study of a literary type.


PRAZ, MARIO. *Machiavelli and the Elizabethans* (1928). A study of the Elizabethan conception of Machiavelli and his influence.


PRIOR, MOODY E. *The Language of Tragedy* (1947). An important book for a study of language in *Tamburlaine*.


RIBNER, IRVING R. *History and Drama in the Age of Shakespeare* (1957).


ROBERTSON, J. M. *Marlowe: A Conspectus* (1931).


SMITH, JAMES. "Marlowe's *Doctor Faustus*," *Scrutiny* VIII (1939-40), 36-55.


SPENCER, THEODORE. *Death and Elizabethan Tragedy* (1936). Spencer maintains that Marlowe was the first dramatist to treat death dramatically.


SPIVACK, BERNARD. *Shakespeare and the Allegory of Evil* (1958). Contains pertinent material on Barabas and the Morality Vice in *The Jew of Malta*.


STEANE, J. B. *Marlowe: A Critical Study* (1964).


WAITH, EUGENE M. *The Herculean Hero in Marlowe, Chapman, Shakespeare, and Dryden* (1962).


WILLEY, BASIL. *The Seventeenth Century Background* (1934).

## SUGGESTED RESEARCH PAPERS

1. Faustus as tragic hero. What do you understand by tragedy? What would be the general conception of tragedy in Marlowe's time? Is Marlowe working within that conception? How does Marlowe construct a tragic universe and how does he make Faustus a tragic figure?

2. Morality play elements in *Doctor Faustus*. What is a morality play and what was its importance in the development of English drama? What specific features, characters, events reveal its influence? How does this affect the structure of the play?

3. The comic portions of *Doctor Faustus*. Which are the comic parts? Why does Marlowe include them? Are they thematically related to the main action? Was there a dramatic tradition for mingling serious and comic matter within the same play? Did Marlowe have a collaborator? If so, does this affect the interpretation of the play?

4. The structure of *Tamburlaine, Part I*. How does Marlowe build the action? Are there sub-plots or minor actions? What are the major themes of the play? How does the action illustrate these themes?

5. Tamburlaine as tragic hero in *Part II*. Study his manner of speech closely and also how events (the death of Zenocrate) affect him. Is Tamburlaine responsible for his "fall"? Is he a "sympathetic" tragic figure or do you feel a sense of justice at his death?

6. Compare and contrast the character of Barabas with that of Abigail in *The Jew of Malta*. Why is Barabas a total villain? What are the ways in which Marlowe makes us aware of this villainy? How does Abigail gain our sympathies? Is she meant to contrast with Barabas, Ithamore, and the others? How do Barabas and Abigail relate to the themes and overall meaning of the play?

7. Marlowe's use of sources in *Edward II*. Read Holinshed's *Chronicles* and some modern accounts of the reign of Edward II. How does Marlowe's account vary from that found in the histories of his own time? What is the modern view of Edward II?

8. Edward II as tragic hero. Is he truly tragic, or is he more a figure of pathos? Why not compare him to Richard II in Shakespeare's *Richard II?*

9. An analysis of Marlowe's life. Gather all the important facts and list the important documents that mention Marlowe. What don't we know about Marlowe? What is needed for fuller information? How does his life relate to his works?

10. Discuss Marlowe's use of blank verse. Study the speech of Faustus to Helen and analyze it closely. What is its dominant imagery? Why does Marlowe use classical references? What is the meter and rhythm of the speech? What is its tone?

# NOTES

# NOTES

# NOTES

# NOTES

# MONARCH
# NOTES *AND STUDY GUIDES*

## *ARE AVAILABLE AT RETAIL STORES EVERYWHERE*

In the event your local bookseller
cannot provide you with other
Monarch titles you want —

# ORDER ON THE FORM BELOW:

Simply send retail price, local
sales tax, if any, plus 35¢ per
book to cover mailing and
handling.

| TITLE # | AUTHOR & TITLE | PRICE |
|---------|----------------|-------|
|  |  |  |
|  |  |  |
|  |  |  |
|  |  |  |
|  |  |  |
|  |  |  |
|  |  |  |
|  |  |  |
|  |  |  |
|  |  |  |
|  |  |  |
|  |  |  |
|  |  |  |
|  | PLUS ADDITIONAL $1.00 PER BOOK FOR POSTAGE |  |
|  | GRAND TOTAL | $ |

*Mail to:* **PRENTICE HALL PRESS,** c/o Simon & Schuster Mail Order Billing, Route 59 at Brook Hill Drive, West Nyack, NY 10994

I enclose $ .......................... to cover retail price, local sales tax, plus mailing and handling. (Make checks payable to Simon & Schuster, Inc.)

Name _____
**(Please print)**
Address _____

City _____ State _____ Zip _____

*Please send check or money order. We cannot be responsible for cash.*